Something Different, Yet the Same

Peggy Adams Fragopoulos

Copyright © 2016 Peggy Adams Fragopoulos

All rights reserved.

ISBN-13-978-1519301680

ISBN-101519301685

DEDICATION

My parents, Paskel and Cora Adams, who raised me with love and first taught me Biblical stories and life lessons. My children, Theologos and Eleni Cora Fragopoulos, who brought an earthly meaning to the word unconditional love. My grandchildren, Alexander, Dimitri, Darius, and Hristina, who have added immeasurable joy to my life and given me the opportunity to revisit my children's childhood. I cannot leave out Teresa and Zach. Also, last but not least, my friends, whom I cannot name individually because I know I would leave someone out, and my FB friends as well as my travel friends, Helen, who goes where I go, and professional colleagues and confidants: Elaine, Frances, Kay, Martha, Marsha, Carolyn, Melissa, Penny, Kathy, Gary, Lowell, and Pokey. I cannot forget Jessie, my first and last to go to with all my print needs and questions.
Thanks, I love all of you!

CONTENTS

1	January	1
2	February	17
3	March	34
4	April	49
5	May	62
6	June	75
7	July	87
8	August	97
9	September	106
10	October	114
11	November	124
12	December	135

Acknowledgments

I want to acknowledge all who have encouraged me to write my Thoughts for the Day in book form. From the time I entered the classroom, I wanted to give my students something to think about, something to take away with them. Throughout my career, I wrote on the board a "thought," either original or otherwise. Currently, Facebook is my mission field.

SOMETHING DIFFERENT, YET THE SAME

January
Thoughts for Each Day

Day 1: Today is a new day and a new beginning. The Lord's mercy and loving-kindness is also new. It does not matter how much we messed up yesterday or last year, God's faithfulness always prevails. As followers, we must wait hopefully and expectantly for God to act in our circumstances because He has promised to do so. "They that wait upon the Lord shall renew their strength; they shall mount up with wings as eagles; they shall run, and not be weary; and they shall walk, and not faint." God knows your every need; trust in Him and Him alone. You are the Apple of His eye. If God had a fridge, your picture would be on it. So, this year, this day is brand new, filled with unlimited possibilities and great expectations. Enjoy! God bless.

Day 2: Doesn't it feel good to really clean house? We throw away the 'science fair project' growing in the fridge, the clutter of paper and boxes we've been saving, the clothes we kept in hopes to fit into them again. (I once pulled out of the closet a 15-year-old skirt and the elastic around the waist had dry-rotted.) Disorder brings negative energy; there's no room for positive action. Paul tells us to 'throw off the past, our former self.' That's right, free yourself of the old and put on the new you. I encourage you to clear out all the 'bag and baggage' of the worrisome past, clean out the clutter in your mind and renew it on God's Word. Both your attitude and your life will be FREE. Clean 'house' today. God bless.

Day 3: Most of us are taught that we can have anything we want in life with effort and courage. I use to struggle with this concept. I might want to be a famous singer but what if, on a scale of 1-10, I am only a 5? Maybe, just maybe, singing is not God's choice for my life. If we transfer our thoughts and our lives to a Christ-centered existence, God will point the way He wants us to go. A ME-centered life will only lead to struggles and ultimate failure. Doing it 'Your Way,' without God, will get you nowhere. You will not feel the joy, the peace, the love, the success of a Christ-centered life. Get away from the "what about me, me, me?" mentality and discover the fullness of life, with everything Christ has available, by choosing a life centered on God's Will for you and you alone. God bless.

Day 4: Do you have people in your life who know your past, and they constantly remind you of your failures, your shortcomings, your mistakes? If possible, cull these individuals out of your life. It's difficult to become your best when you are surrounded with negative energy. It is important that those around you see the "fruits" of the spirit that you bear (love joy, peace, patience, kindness, goodness, faithfulness, and self control). Forget what individuals say; it's more important what God says. What's awesome is God throws away our 'sins' (mistakes) as far as the east is from the west and He remembers them no more. Don't be discouraged with those constant negative reminders of your flaws; instead, encourage yourself in the Lord by looking how far you have come in your journey with God. God bless.

Day 5: Fear is a natural emotion but do you let it get in the way of living your life? Are there dreams you have for your future but fear and doubt cloud the way? The very act of pressing forward through those feelings will slay whatever monsters hide in your imagination. The way to eliminate fear in life is to never get out of your comfort zone. If you do this, you will remain where you are and you will never grow and achieve your dream or fulfill God's Will for your life. I challenge you to push those negative imaginings aside, get out of your comfort zone and fear itself will loosen its hold on you. Courage will take the place of fear in your heart; and most importantly, you will achieve your dreams. God bless.

Day 6: Most first-time parents cannot visualize the overwhelming role they will play in their children's lives. The Bible tells us to "Train up a child in the way he should go: and when he is old, he will not depart from it." And we try. Parents make choices, which they believe to be the 'right-choice' for that particular time; however, many of us can look back and realize those decisions were perhaps wrong decisions. I remember putting shoes on my children at an early age and now they say that is the wrong thing to do. I also fed them Similac and now we know breast milk is better. I told my children they were lucky to have made it to adulthood. Did we make these choices selfishly or were they made because that was what seemed to be the right choice at the time? Sure, we have make mistakes BUT our children still grow up, and they become responsible for their own decisions. At this point in their lives, we need to let Go and let God take control. Our most powerful tool is prayer, letting God work in our children's lives. Remember, you and your children are equally God's children and He loves us all. God knows what to do with that young, independent adult when we, as parents, have no idea. Trust Him. God bless.

Day 7: Forgiveness and Patience changes your life and makes negative situations turn around. When someone holds on to hurts and offenses, such as in a marriage, wounds cannot be healed and love is compromised. Real love shows mercy and forgives. Love gives other people another chance. Even though major hurts may exist, you must decide to release control and let God heal your broken spirit. Bitterness and resentment will poison your own life as well as ALL of the lives around you. Pray for the strength to forgive. Ask God for help and concentrate on the good in your life rather than the negative. In time, all is forgiven and you are free. God bless.

Day 8: Good and evil surrounds us. God is never behind the evil which persists in the world so don't blame Him. But you can blame the devil for many things because he came to steal, kill, and destroy. He brings deception; he introduces lies, deceit, hatred, and envy into our lives. He wants us to doubt God's goodness. However, sometimes the bad that happens is of our own making. We make wrong choices; we choose to be disrespectful, lying, sinful individuals. This brings destruction on ourselves and affects those that we love. Remember - we do reap what we sow. Use prayer to get closer to God because only He has the Power to help us in ALL things. In other words, "Cling to a good God in a bad world." "Just pray and God will be on the way." ~ inspired Bobby Davis. God bless.

Day 9: Purposeful, relentless, unwavering, determined - this attitude is what carries you through life. You started out that way: you were determined to crawl, walk, talk, learn to ride a bike, drive. . . Determination has aided you throughout your life, and it is the factor in your human makeup, which will enable you to obtain your dream. A determined attitude helps you make a commitment to reach your goal. Feed your determination with belief in yourself and belief in God. Make Plan A to reach your goal, but don't make a Plan B. Be resolved to see Plan A to the finish. The journey will be well worth it. Your behavior, (kindness, humility, and a service attitude) will propel you to success. Set your path today and be determined to see it to maturity. You will be energized each day until you achieve your dream and remember, you are never too old to begin. (inspired by R. Byrne) God bless.

Day 10: Never take yourself too seriously. – "Pride cometh before the fall. - Don't think more highly of yourself than you ought. . . . "All of these Thoughts came to me yesterday after I posted a quote on my FB account. I soon realized my voice-message had changed the first word from Thought to a 4-letter word that I had bragged the day before that I had never used. I had a few readers who were on the ball, including a call from my son who had been called by a friend to inform me of my error. I frantically tried to correct it but I could not figure it out since I had posted it on my phone. My friend Penny came to my aid and I resent a corrected 'thought.' God definitely has a sense of humor and a way to humble us. I learned my lesson. Tread carefully in voice messaging today and everyday. God bless.

Day 11: One of the greatest battles for the human being is the fight to maintain the right attitude. You never see James Bond complaining or Superman whining or Indiana Jones blaming others for his lot in life. We never want to see our superheroes with such a negative, cynical, weak attitude. *Those who maintain an optimistic outlook about life have the mind of a hero. Your attitude will either lift you to success or will leave you in the ditches of life. Use this incredible tool to realize your dreams and to live the life God wants you to live. - inspired by R. Byrne. God bless

Day 12: Ultimately to achieve anything in life you must believe that you can achieve it. You need to believe that all things are possible. Your belief in yourself and your belief in God's ability through you can carry you throughout your life. It will propel you over every difficult situation or through every storm that you face and ultimately, it will enable you to achieve your dreams. If you do not believe in yourself, change your thinking. Begin to have faith that you can achieve. If you change your way of thinking, you can change your life. God bless

Day 13: Belief in God gives us hope. We live our lives with the assurance of God's promises. As we put flowers on our family and friends' graves, we can look forward to meeting them in the future. . . ."to be absent from the body, and to be present with the Lord.." How sad it is to not believe, to have no hope. May God give you peace and the assurance that He is with you always, even to the ends of the earth and He is a God who cannot lie. You must only believe. God bless.

Day 14: As parents, we are concerned about raising 'good' children who will become responsible, kind, and loving adults. We provide nutritious food, we encourage exercise (sports, other activities) that the body needs in order to remain healthy; we also 'demand' schooling which will prepare them intellectually, academically and with skills that will enable them to make a living and be accountable adults . . . but what about their 'spirits'? Each individual knows there's more to us than flesh, blood, and bones, but we have many questions. As parents, our greatest responsibility is to guide our children into the knowledge of 'God,' 'a Supreme Being,' an 'Almighty Creator.' An understanding of 'God' gives them a purpose, and they will understand they are part of the whole, not just the material aspect, which will fade away. *Parents, don't forget to minister to your 'spirit man' and to 'direct' your children in the way of the Lord. Their 'eternal' life depends on it. God bless.

Day 15: What is love? The following Shakespearean sonnet gives a great definition: "Let me not to the marriage of true minds Admit impediments (limitations). Love is not love Which alters (changes) when it alteration finds, Or bends with the remover to remove: O no; it is an ever-fixed mark, (constant) That looks on tempests (storms), and is never shaken; It is the star to every wandering bark (ship), Whose worth's unknown, although his height be taken. Love's not Time's fool, though rosy lips and cheeks Within his bending sickle's compass come; (appearance changes/not love) Love alters not with his brief hours and weeks, But bears it out even to the edge of doom. If this be error and upon me proved, I never writ, nor no man ever loved." ~ Shakespeare *LOVE doesn't alter just because he gets Dunlap disease: his gut done lapped over his belt or she can't get rid of the 15 pounds gained while birthing their child; or she/he has been diagnosed with a horrible illness. No, It is CONSTANT. It is a choice day-by-day to exhibit LOVE in word and deed. God bless.

Day 16: Many people should have been born with their eyes in the back of their heads; that is the way they live their lives. They are looking at life through a rear-view mirror. Definitely, we learn from our past, but we are to move on - live in the Present. We can never redo, recreate, or undo the past, but we do have a wonderful today; and we should know that we can 'plan' and move toward our future. Quit playing the 'blame' game, the 'if only' 'should of,' 'could of,' 'would of' games of the past. Instead, play "I will take full responsibility' and 'my future-my choice' game of the here and NOW. "One problem with gazing too frequently into the past is that we may turn around to find" our future has run out of time. ~ Michael Cibenko. Enjoy today! Give thanks! Plan for tomorrow! God bless!

Day 17: Some people think they must be perfect in order to be used by God. Not so, my friend. If we are flawed then, for sure, we can be called to carry God's Word to the world. Look at the many examples in the Bible, the greatest being Paul, who had previously put Christians to death before He had a God encounter and then became one of God's greatest tools in spreading the gospel. Don't compare yourself to others; look into God's mirror; "you are uniquely and wonderfully made" to serve God where He places you. Our weaknesses can become our greatest weapon in the war against evil. No one else can be called to do what you have been called to do. Step up and step out, no matter how imperfect you may see yourself, and discover where and how God wants to use you. God bless.

Day 18: "Here is a test to find whether your mission on earth is finished. If you're alive, it isn't." ~ Richard Bach. No one has a perfect life. We tend to think that some people do, this is mostly determined by the money and fame individuals possess, but that is not a good measurement. For example, the Kennedy family had multiple tragedies: two sons assassinated, one killed in the war, a mentally challenged daughter, another daughter who chocked to death, the tragic air death of 'John John' (as many Americans called him). Life isn't perfect, even for the rich and famous. *If I am in a public place, I often wonder what each person's life story is. We would all be surprised at the difficulties others have faced. I encourage you today to live each day, whatever the challenge. Be an over-comer with God's help. Jesus came that we might "have life and have it more abundantly." Look for life's opportunities today - you just might discover your mission while here on earth. God bless.

Day 19: Do you choose what goes into your mind? or do you just let anything in? I remember my sister taking me to the drive-in when I was 9 (the first movie I ever saw) - the lead female was pregnant. She died, as well as the baby, in childbirth. Many years have passed and I still remember the fear that attacked my mind that night, and it stayed with me through the birth of my own children. Recently, I read about a teenage school shooter who played 67 different video games; 49 of which contained extreme violence. *It IS important to choose wisely what is downloaded into your mind and spirit and into the hearts and lives of your children. These decisions may affect your/their thoughts, actions, and choices the rest of your/their lives. Instead, download Biblical principles, which give 'life' into one's spirit. God bless.

Day 20: Who out there amongst you are both intelligent and wise? It should be evident by your noble living shown forth in your 'good' works, free of jealousy/envy, rivalry, selfish ambition, falsity to the Truth, disharmony, confusion and vile practices. The Fruit God is looking for is conformity to His will in Thought and Deed. When God's Will is done, wisdom is obvious and the harvest of 'good' fruits is plentiful - Wisdom from above is undefiled, peace-loving, courteous, considerate, gentle, willing to yield to others, full of compassion and 'good' fruits (behavior), free of doubt, wavering, and insincerity. . . What a great world this would be! (Look for evidence of your good fruit today). God bless.

Day 21: Marriages split; friendships disintegrate; families break apart - Why? Many times it is because someone does not have control over his/her tongue. The Bible says that the tongue (like the rudder of a ship or the bit in a horse's mouth) is a small member of the body but it has great power. It is restless, evil, and full of deadly poison. It also tells us that no man can tame the tongue but you CAN turn it over to God and ask for His help in controlling this "fire" that with its spark can set a forest a blaze. Once again, there is life and death in the power of the tongue - speak life into your marriages, friendships, families, and work place. James 3. God bless.

Day 22: Faith comes by hearing and hearing by the Word of God. This is a major reason to read God's Word and attend church or other spirit-filled gatherings. Faith is shown by the words you speak and the actions you take. Our prayers are seeds, which we plant when we pray. After we say, "AMEN," don't dig your seed up by the negative words you say (my prayer will never be answered; or so much time has passed and nothing has happened). Instead, continue to believe and demonstrate that belief. "Thank you, God, that you are working on my request" (remember, many times other people are involved in your prayers and everything has to come together at the right moment in time) We have free will. God will not MAKE someone go against his/her will. Take action to demonstrate faith: if you are praying for rain, take an umbrella when you go out. If you have asked

God for a baby, buy something for that baby. Faith is Kingdom currency. It is impossible to please God without it. Be rich in faith. Spend a little 'faith currency' today. God bless.

Day 23: A small pebble in one's shoe can cause death. How? A pebble results in a bruise, which can become a sore, later an infection, over time a 'cancer' poisoning the blood, and eventual death. Is this an extreme? Not really, because this is also the way 'small' sin enters our lives. We think it is hidden, nobody knows; but as time passes, it can destroy our reputations, our relationships, our 'world' as we know it. What price are you willing to pay for those 'small' indiscretions. There's no exception, we will reap what we sow and most times, it is a 'bumper crop'. Therefore, we need to judge ourselves, (remove the pebble) and we will not be judged. God bless.

Day 24: Are your ears garbage dumps for your family and friends to fill? Does it then effect your attitude, viewpoint, stance, and reaction toward others and things in your life? Maybe we need to guard what we permit others to unload upon us. *When I first moved to Greece, I was invited to meet with a group of International Women who were living in Greece. I only attended two meetings. Why? All they did was gripe and complain about what Greece did not have. I knew I would never be happy in my new home if I joined that group. I encourage each one of you to beware of the poisonous attitude of gossip, grumbling, and discontent. Let

God help you filter the garbage that is flung your way. God bless.

Day 25: Are you a murderer? Do you assassinate people with your tongue? Do you slaughter the character of friends, family, and those you don't even know? The Bible tells us: "Watch out that no poisonous root of bitterness grows up to trouble you." Envy, jealousy, lack in one's own life can cause bitterness toward others. *The power of 'life' and 'death' is in the tongue. If you have a problem with "diarrhea of the mouth," pray that God will work in you to get rid of the poisonous root embedded in your life and 'stinkin up your environment'. Take care, otherwise, you will be destroyed by your own poison. God bless.

Day 26: Self control is the ability to control one's emotions, behavior, and desires. The Bible describes it as one of the fruits of the spirit. *Do your emotions rule over you or do you have self restraint and control over them? One look at the evening news or the newspaper, we can see where emotions rule to the point of disaster and even death. If you are "throwing one of your fits" and someone (a boss, close friend, pastor) knocks on your door, how quickly would you gain control of your "out of control" self? Most likely, you would put on a new face and obtain a new demeanor in the 'blink of an eye.' Exercise self control in ALL things. A person out-of-control is out of the will of God. God bless.

Day 27: Many people are concerned about leaving a legacy of money, real estate, personal property, or scholarships in their names when they leave this earth. However, the very best legacy one can leave is a life lived with honor, dignity, love, forgiveness, service, and honesty. Be that person everyone can depend on; a person who is a man/woman of his/her word. In fact, we don't have to die to leave this kind of legacy; we can live it day-by-day. It's one thing to leave an inheritance of money, real estate holdings, and a substantial stock portfolio, but it is entirely another to leave a light of "goodness" burning brightly to show others the way. This kind of inheritance is "priceless." God bless.

Day 28: If you don't like yourself, you need to get over it because no matter where you go, you are there. You are created by the Master Himself, and He has a divine plan for your life. "The one thing you have that nobody else has is You. Your voice, your mind, your story, your vision. So write and draw and build and play and dance and live as only you can." ~ Neil Gaiman *Give God the glory for all He has done for you and learn to love yourself and live a life of excellence in Jesus's name. God bless.

Day 29: Today is a new day and a new beginning. The Lord's mercy and loving-kindness is also new today. It does not matter how much we messed up yesterday, God's faithfulness prevails. As followers, we must wait hopefully and expectantly for God to act in our circumstances because He has promised to do so. "They that wait upon the Lord shall renew their strength; they shall mount up with wings as eagles; they shall run, and not be weary; and they shall walk, and not faint." God knows your every need; trust in Him and Him alone. You are the Apple of His eye. If He had an iPhone, your picture would be on the cover. So, this year/month/day is brand new, filled with endless possibilities and great expectations. Enjoy! God bless.

Day 30: Success gained by deceit, trickery, and fraud is at first sweet; but afterwards, one's mouth will be filled with gravel . . . and one's gut will fill with ulcers of failure and defeat. Stress will bring your collapse. Remember, liars must have good memories. You WILL get caught in your own trap of deception. Live the truth each and every day! If you do, your worries will be few and you won't have to keep good notes. God bless.

Day 31: "If a man is called to be a street sweeper, he should sweep streets even as Michelangelo painted, or Beethoven composed music or Shakespeare wrote poetry. He should sweep streets so well that all the hosts of heaven and earth will pause to say, 'Here lived a great street sweeper who did his job well." Martin Luther King Jr. *Excellence is available to all human beings, but accepted by only a few. Do you strive for excellence? If not, begin today. God bless.

February

Thoughts for Each Day

Day 1: Show no prejudice, no partiality, no snobbery. (Bible) Do you pay more attention to the rich or to those in authority - giving them the best 'seat,' catering to their desires while you neglect or even show contempt for the poor of this world. God commands us to "love your neighbor as yourself." Because if you show prejudice, favoritism for one more than the other, it is a 'sin.' Don't love with wrong motives, but love equally and "do unto (all) others as you would have them to do unto you." Have a blessed day and may the favor of Almighty God be upon you. God bless.

Day 2: Quit making excuses for your bad behavior. Quit playing the blame game: I am the way I am because of my mother, father, sister, brother, teacher, etc. Quit saying, "That's just who I am." The Bible says if we become followers of Jesus: "This means that anyone who belongs to Christ has become a NEW person. The old life is gone; a new life has begun!" *We will live very miserable lives if we refuse to let God work in us. We must be willing to be led by the Spirit of God and CHANGE to become like Jesus Himself. Only then can we be transformed into new creatures and live a victorious life in Christ Jesus. God bless.

Day 3: Recently my grandchildren had heard a minister say that there's nothing in this world 'for' them. The children were very confused. They love life: sports, travel, amusements - like most people. It is not only children who are sometimes confused. So, what does that statement mean? "God came that we may have and enjoy life and have it in abundance until it overflows." So evidently, there's something here for us. And while we are making choices and living our lives, we are to live it with love for all mankind, showing God's goodness in all that we do (including sports, entertainment, work, fellowship, and church). By LIVING and walking in God's love, we are influencing others to believe and accept Jesus as their Savior. Yes, there is something for us here. We have a monumental commission (purpose) while here on earth. We need to take it seriously while we live and enjoy the life God has given us. God bless.

Day 4: A lifeguard is one who brings another to safety, he/she performs rescues and saves lives; in fact, a lifeguard is part of emergency services. Are you equipped to be a lifeguard? Have you had your training? I'm talking about our role as a lifeguard for those around us: our children, parents, friends, even strangers. However, there's more than saving a physical life, there's a spiritual life that lives for eternity. Are you doing your part to secure the future for those you love. Be a lifeguard for God. The BIBLE is your training manual. Take time to study and be well trained for all emergencies. Guard those around you with diligence and begin training them to become lifeguards for eternity. Have an awesome week. God bless.

Day 5: One of the most difficult times in life is when we are attacked by sickness and disease. Let's look at what the Bible says about healing. "He sends forth His Word and heals them and rescues them . . ." If you are sick or anyone around you is sick, look up Bible scriptures about healing and commit them to memory, meditate upon them, repeat them - saying "I will not be overcome by sickness or disease. I will trust God to comfort, strengthen, heal, and restore my life as I walk in His will." J. Meyer *Encourage yourself with His Word and with testimonies of previous victories. (At 18 mos. I had polio; doctors said I would not make it, but I am still here. At 30, I had cervical cancer, but I am still here) God is merciful: Seek Him, Believe Him, Trust Him! God bless.

Day 6: "Be quick to hear and slow to speak, slow to take offense and slow to get angry; man's anger does not promote the righteousness of God" *God's Word planted deep in our hearts has the power to not only save our souls but to control our emotions and temptations. ~James 1 *What a wonderful world this would be if everyone would abide by this advice. We can start in our own homes and with our own 'world.' Don't forget to bridle your tongue and move unhurriedly to feel resentment today and every day. God bless.

Day 7: Shakespeare, thru Hamlet's voice, instructs his mother: "Go not to mine uncle's bed . . . refrain tonight, and that shall lend a kind of easiness to the next abstinence, the next 'even' more easy." The Bible states if we fall into temptation and overcome, it is a test of our faith; we then develop endurance and steadfastness; afterwards we will be perfect and fully developed. *Concealing 'sin' will eat you up from the inside. Rejecting 'sin' (one temptation at a time) will build a strong, Christlike nature, which is pleasing into to Lord. Your life will be peaceful and filled with joy. God bless.

Day 8: Many of us are waiting for God to do 'something' in our lives. We're waiting for a major breakthrough, the next miracle, a windfall of blessings, prayers to be answered. We know we must keep the faith; however, faith is the belief of things that are not seen and sometimes this causes us to become discouraged. But we must believe . . . on and on and on. Nevertheless, there IS something else that must be done: we must put our 'natural' to God's 'super' in order for the supernatural to show up. Remember? Moses had to hold out the staff and THEN God divided the Red Sea. In prison, Paul and Silas began to sing praises to God and THEN the gates opened. Esther approached the king (which meant death if he did not receive her) THEN God saved her people (the Jews). Ask yourself, what are you NOT doing? Ask God if there is an action you need to take in the 'natural' so He can put His 'super' on it. YOUR "Supernatural" miracle is right around the corner. Believe it, speak it, see it in your spirit, put action to it and God will do the rest. God bless.

Day 9: Yesterday, I told you that God can take our chaotic lives and bring order and purpose. How does that happen? If we aim ourselves to follow Jesus, He will communicate with us. As we become more sensitive to His voice, we will recognize His counseling and guidance as we live our lives. For example, this past weekend I made a comment (before thinking) and I felt inside that I should NOT have said what I did. That √ in my spirit was God's correction. As we become more responsive to God's urgings, our lives become more Christlike. When do we arrive? Never! There will always be areas in which we can improve. Hebrews 13:20-21 contains a wonderful prayer you can add to your prayer life: "May the God of peace strengthen/perfect and make me what I should be and equip me with everything good so that I may carry out God's Will while He works in me and accomplishes that which is pleasing in His sight, through Jesus Christ." May God's blessings and favor be yours today and every day.

Day 10: Do you ever feel that you are such a mess that there's no hope? You have made so many mistakes, there's no way to correct all of your wrong choices? Let God take your mess and make it His masterpiece. No one expects you to go from despicable you to sainthood overnight. However, if you put your 'clay' into His capable hands, He can mold your life into a thing of beauty. "Like clay in the hands of the Potter, so are you in 'His' hands." Let the Master do His work on you. God bless.

Day 11: As many head to church on Sunday or whatever may be planned for the Sabbath, I want to remind each of you that you can produce 'good' fruit wherever you go. We go to church to worship God, give thanks, and learn more about His divine Word; however, it is in our everyday life, in ordinary circumstances that we bare the fruit of our salvation. The Bible tells us, we are known by the fruit that we bare. What kind of fruit are you producing? If we are wearing the label of Christianity, our fruit should look like the following: charity (love), kindness, mercy, joy, generosity, service. And it should be evident, not just when we feel like it, but at ALL times. So today and every day, go out and bare 'good' fruit and give plentifully to all. Show the world that we are His people, not wolves in sheep's clothing. God bless.

Day 12: "I want my life to be something more than long." ("Corner of the Sky") We have the opportunity to make a difference each and every new day. We can impact the world in which we live. We should live so someone will shed a tear when we have passed and also rejoice because we have been here. Think today what you would like your legacy to be and take steps toward reaching it. *I want to make a difference; how about you? God bless.

Day 13: When you open the paper or listen to the news, you wonder if peace will ever reign on this earth even though Jesus came for us to have peace. "These things I have spoken to you, that in Me you might have peace. In the world you shall have tribulation: but be of good cheer; I have overcome the world." Jimi Hendrix said it this way, "When the power of love overcomes the love of power, the world will know peace." Simply said but what a powerful statement! Let's begin at home with family, at play with friends, at work with coworkers, and in public with strangers - peace CAN win if we CAN become people who are motivated by love. I love you, my readers. God bless.

Day 14: I know many of you want to eliminate stress from your lives; however, 'Johnny' has soccer practice 5 days a week and tournaments on the weekend, 'Little Bit' takes piano twice a week and has soccer practice once a week, a game on the weekend and she's also in beginning dance. We must not forget the homework, which in many households, parents must help in order to finish by bedtime. The rest are leaving it up to the kids because the homework has passed the parent's expertise. I've not even touched on the hours of work done by the parents and the many who must bring work home with them. Cooking, cleaning, caring for aged parents, shopping, washing clothes, and the list goes on and on. You know the drill. Your blood pressure is off the charts! Other medical issues are rearing their ugly heads and we are suppose to have time to work out? WHAT'S A FELLOW/GAL TO DO? *If this sounds like your schedule or somewhat similar, remember YOU make your schedule. It is time to prune 'time.' Put necessities first. Jesus tells us "He came so we might have peace.- Let not your hearts be troubled, neither let them be afraid - be anxious for nothing." He did not say to run ourselves into an early grave. We have a brain, let's use it! Simplify your life and begin to live in peace, not stress. God bless.

Day 15: Even though my family was considered poor when I was growing up, we had a formal living room that was only used two or three times a year for special occasions. Also, Mom had collected the 'good' China by obtaining one place setting at a time when it was given away by the local bank. Finally, it reached a 12-place setting, and we never used it, but we had it, just in case, and it looked good in the China cabinet. When Mom died, she had several new gowns, never worn, in case she went to the hospital. I would venture to say, many of you can identify with this story. *Are you the same way? We are each designed for a specific purpose, but just like these items, we live out our lives never fulfilling what we were created for. In our hearts, we have desires and dreams. Could those dreams possibly be our purpose? "I know the thoughts and plans I have for you" said the Lord. If you are living out your purpose, your life will have meaning and you will experience joy unspeakable. Talk to God today if you are like these unused items. Discover your purpose - God's plan for your life. Don't sit around collecting dust, but live a 'burnished' life of use. God bless.

Day 16: Are you ruled by money? Are the Jacksons, Franklins, and Grants clogging your arteries, stifling your relationships, and destroying your God connection? Is enough never enough? No matter what the economy looks like or what your bank account may say, if you will trust in the Lord, He will find a way to bring you through your greatest financial difficulties. "I have never seen the righteous forsaken or their children begging bread."~ Psalms. He has promised to "supply all our needs according to His riches in glory." Learn to trust Him for your every need. Seek Him (not the dollar), obey His Word (not society's) and trust Him (not your broker) to provide whatever it is you need and you WILL NOT be disappointed. God bless.

Day 17: If you are a Christ follower, you are seated with Jesus at the right hand of God the Father. What does that mean? It means that the same power which raised Jesus from the grave is at work in you to raise you up out of whatever earthly grave you are in or whatever garbage pile that is trying to bury you. Shake off debt, defeat, sickness, discouragement, depression, disappointment, worry, anxiety, unhappiness, hatred, envy, jealousy, temptation . . .Jesus overcame the grave so you and I will be over-comers. We need only to have 'faith' and speak 'out of our mouths' that we are Victorious in Christ Jesus. *DON'T speak the problem; SPEAK the victory. Pray: "Whatever problem I may be facing today, I will live with the confidence that God will help me overcome it." God bless.

Day 18: First things first! Make a list of your daily activities. Now, categorize them according to their importance. (some of you may know this parable but it bears repeating) Choose a rock for each activity - big rocks for those most important and medium rocks for those less important that may be put off until later like washing dishes. Finally, use sand for all of the tiny activities such as playing video games, talking on the phone, and watching TV. Then get a half gallon mason jar. Think about what you spend most of your day doing and put in the appropriate rocks. Many of you may fill your jar with sand and then you do not have any room for the things that really need to be done. Your largest rock should be to spend time with God, reading your Bible and praying. If you start your day with that activity and continue to put the large rocks (those things most important) and then the smaller rocks - there WILL still be room for the sand. those small minute, sometimes unnecessary but fun activities. If you put the sand first, there is no room for much of anything else. Remember, each day to put "first things first." God will bless you and His favor will be upon you. God bless.

Day 19: The Bible tells us that temptations to do wrong will come. Who presents these temptations? Could it be you? Sin always looks attractive, but in reality sins are snares and traps, which are set to trip us up. Did you know the Bible hands out strong warnings about the person or people who set the traps, causing God's believers to fall? It says "woe" (grievous distress/affliction/trouble) will come to those who cause others to sin. In fact, the Bible says, "it would be more profitable if a millstone were hung around his neck and he be hurled into the sea than he should cause others to sin." You may say "that's not me. I've never offered anyone drugs or alcohol. I've not caused others to lie or cheat or steal." It could be something as 'innocent' as wearing clothes that cause the sin of lust. The way we handle anger may cause out-of-control wrath to those around us. *Let's do as the Bible suggests – examine and judge ourselves as well as our behavior so we will not be judged by God. God Bless.

Day 20: The Lord is our provider and we are not to fear because He shall supply all of our needs. We must learn to trust God in all areas of our lives, including finances. However, the Bible does say, "whoever is unwilling to work, shall not eat." Pray each day for your needs to be met and for God to give you enough that you may bless others. Pray for His Almighty favor to be upon your life. In addition, we need to be wise caretakers of our money: give some, save some, and spend some. If we keep a balance, we will prosper and be in good health just as our soul prospers. Our financial blessings and health are tied to the prosperity of our souls. It is necessary for us to work out our salvation (learning His Word and obeying it) and then our souls will prosper. His Word gives us the choice: life or death; blessings or curses. I encourage you to choose life and God's blessings will be with you all the way, every day. God bless.

Day 21: Sometimes, I am running late and I question myself: am I usually late for appointments or doing what others expect me to do? *While living in Greece, I came to anticipate everyone to run late. If they said 8, it usually meant 9, 9:30, or maybe 10. It drove me crazy!! Instead of falling into their pattern of time, I made it even more a priority to be on time. It is a pet peeve of mine, even today. Are you punctual, observant of the appointed time? Charles Dickens said: "I never could have done what I have done without the habits of punctuality, order, and diligence." "Better three hours too soon than one minute too late," quipped my beloved William Shakespeare. ~ Have you missed out because of tardiness? Break the habit; be on time. God is never late and you certainly don't want Him to be. God bless.

Day 22: When we are babies learning to walk, we take many tumbles but EVERY baby will try again. They are encouraged by their family but their own desire is strong; they will pull themselves up and go again. As we get older, we lose that youthful zeal, desire, and determination to get up and try again. We might not make it, we might get hurt, someone might laugh, - we make all kinds of excuses. But no matter the age, we still have some noble work to be done. The poet Tennyson says "Tis not too late to seek a newer world" . . . . we must continue as long as we have life - "to strive, to seek, to find, and not to yield" to age, to fear, or to laziness. So get up, brush yourself off, push forward and keep trying - you just might succeed. God bless.

Day 23: Free Will is a belief that touches nearly everything we value. Law, politics, religion, public policy, intimate relationships, morality—as well as feelings of remorse or personal achievement—all are governed by free will. Every person is the source of his or her thoughts and actions. ~ inspired by Sam Harris. It is true, we make choices and we reap what we sow. But we also reap what other people sow. This concept is sometimes difficult to swallow. *The solution to living a peaceful life in spite of the situations that are out of our control is to seek God. He has promised to give us peace and joy. For those things in our control make wise choices and for those things out of our control, depend upon God's protection and guidance. God bless.

Day 24: . . . there is hope for your future. ~ Bible *You CAN begin again. You CAN start over. "Hope deferred makes the heart sick, but when the desire is fulfilled, it is a tree of life." ~ Prov. We need to take action. We cannot sit back and wait for success, health, relationships, and promotion to fall on us while we play video games and watch TV. It is never too late to STOP procrastinating, complaining, and blaming. Decide you this day to begin again . . . to step out and find out just how much your hard work and God's ability can accomplish in your life. May God's favor be upon you. God bless.

Day 25: Do not be so deceived and misled! Evil relationships corrupt and deprave good manners and morals and character. ~ 1 Cor.15:33 Ask God for the wisdom to choose correct people to be in relationship with. "Do you not know that being the world's friend is being God's enemy." James 4:4. Surround yourself with people who will encourage you and come alongside you in your walk with the Lord. To maintain a healthy spiritual life, take care whom you are in company with, what you choose to read, to watch, to do. These choices will help determine the level of God you have in your life. God bless.

Day 26: Once a friend told me how busy he was. He had a Deacon's meeting on Monday; choir practice on Tuesday; prayer meeting on Wednesday; Thursday was visitation; and Friday was a church financial meeting; and church on

Sunday. I asked him when he spent time with his family - he had two young children. He had a confused expression on his face. *My point is that sometimes we are soooo BUSY doing God's Work, we are not spending any time with Him. In the Bible, Jesus went away to spend time with God after every healing, meeting, or teaching in order to replenish Himself. Before we go out to DO; we need to spend time and BE with God. Our family and others we encounter will know when we have spent time with the Lord. **And just maybe, we also need to rework our schedules/our commitments because God expects us to spend time with our families also. God Bless.

Day 27: Do you communicate with God each day? Read the Bible? Meditate on God's Word? Pray and give thanks to God? He wants to hear from you. If you are a parent, nothing is better than your child hugging, kissing, calling you - it doesn't matter the age. Don't you think God feels the same? And like a parent, He wants to be there for you, to provide for you, to bless you. Prayer is building a rapport (relationship) with God. Prayer is communication, not just on your part but also waiting to hear what God places on your heart. He wants to be a part of your whole life, not just your morning church service. Talk to God as you would talk to a friend. He is a friend like no other, and He has the power to help us more than anyone else. Try it today. He is waiting. God bless.

Day 28: "I believe in Christianity as I believe that the sun has risen: not because I see it but because of it, I see everything else." C. S. Lewis *Lewis was once an atheist, but realized how very wrong he was. You may be at a stage in life where you do not believe but if you search for an answer, God will reveal Himself to you, just like He revealed Himself to Lewis. Billy Graham reminds us all: "Other appointments in life we can neglect or break, but death is an appointment that no man can ignore, no man can break." Be ready! For a Believer, "Death is not a period but a comma in the story of life." ~ A. Tarver. If not before, I hope to see you after the comma. God bless.

Day 29: Peter had a real-life miracle when he walked on water, heading toward Jesus . . . "But when he saw the wind, he was afraid and, beginning to sink, cried out, "Lord, save me!" He did not begin to sink until he looked at the adverse circumstances around him - the water was rough, the wind was fierce and no one, except Jesus, had walked on water. *If Peter had kept his focus on the Lord, he would not have sunk. Isn't that what happens in our lives? We become afraid, we take our eyes off Jesus and we sink into our fears. Peter only had to cry out to Jesus, and the Lord extended his hand and saved him. God wants to live in our day-to-day; He wants us to keep our eyes upon Him, never wavering. He has promised to be with us always, so what is there to fear? Through your life's storms and your daily

SOMETHING DIFFERENT, YET THE SAME

trails, just keep your eyes on the Master - He never takes His eyes off of you. God

March

Thoughts for Each Day

Day 1: Sloth/laziness is considered one of the 7 deadly sins. Sloth is defined as spiritual or emotional apathy (absence or suppression of passion, emotion, or excitement), neglecting what God has spoken, and being physically an emotionally inactive. Does this describe YOU? The Bible tells us that "Diligent hands will rule, but laziness ends in slave labor" - "The soul of the lazy man desires and has nothing; but the soul of the diligent shall be made rich" It is my belief that even parents do not correct their children because it takes effort and many or just too slothful to be bothered. Sometimes we are lazy because we are physically and emotionally unhealthy. Depression, or mere sadness, can sap you of energy, motivation, strength and health. Choose today to take charge of yourself. Self-discipline involves acting according to what you think instead of how you feel in the moment. Take steps to become physically healthy and read God's Word to help you become emotionally and spiritually healthy. Don't come to the end of your life and realize that you have not because of your slothful lifestyle. God bless.

Day 2: Don't think of yourself more highly than you ought to think. ~ Romans 12:3 Nothing is so hard to do gracefully as getting down off your high horse. ~ Franklin Jones. We are no better than the homeless man/woman sleeping in the back alley and going through the trash, trying to find food. Our lives are wrapped in choices and opportunities. Each of us can make a bad decision which will have devastating consequences. I encourage you to look at others through God's eyes, not from the top of your horse looking down. Have mercy (kindness/forgiveness) toward others because God shows mercy toward us. Have an awesome day. God bless.

Day 3: John Milton wrote, "The mind is its own place and in itself can make a Heaven of hell, a hell of Heaven." *What have you been thinking? It's important! If we think about eating an ice cream and keep meditating on it, it will not be long until we go get ice cream (for me, it is Pralines and Cream) "Your power is in your Thoughts, so stay awake. In other words, remember to remember." ~ The Secret. "Fix your Thoughts on what is true, and honorable, and right, and pure, and lovely, and admirable. Think about things that are excellent and worthy of praise." ~ Bible - Do Not forget the strength of your Thoughts because they become actions and those actions determine your future. God bless.

Day 4: You are to put on the new self, created to be like God in true righteousness and holiness. ~ Eph. 4:24 We cannot put on a new nature if we clothe ourselves each day in yesterday's disappointments, past hurts, bygone sorrows, deferred hopes, former defeats. We must let go of our frustrations and failures. Once we do that and put on the vim, vigor, and vitality of God's Word, we will move on to Victory in Christ Jesus. If you are already dressed in your old self today, change - right now - and put on your new self. You will never want the 'old clothes' again. God bless.

Day 5: He gives power to the weak and strength to the powerless. Those who trust in the Lord will find new strength. They will soar high on wings like eagles. They will run and not grow weary. They will walk and not faint. *These are more of God's promises that we MUST learn to stand on and have faith in. *I remember thinking that what was going on in my life was impossible to live through. But I am still here! Take a moment to think back on your past & revisit the victories. God will ALWAYS be with you. He will NEVER forsake you. Encourage yourself and build your faith day by day on God's promises. God bless.

Day 6: How many of us throw our children aside and refuse a relationship with them because they did something wrong. Do we look at them and declare how imperfect they are and tell them to get out of our sight. I certainly hope not. *I am here to tell you that God does NOT cast us aside when we mess up. In Proverbs we are told "He that covers his sins shall not prosper: but whoso confesses and forsakes them shall have mercy." All we have to do is fess up when we mess up and "he is faithful and just to forgive us our sins, and to cleanse us from ALL unrighteousness." Don't try to punish yourself and feel you are unworthy - Jesus's death on the cross is big enough to cast our sins as far as the east is from the west. STOP beating yourself up. God's mercy is always available for the asking. God bless.

Day 7: God has promises for each of us who believe. "For I know the plans I have for you," says the Lord. "They are plans for good and not for disaster, to give you a future and a hope." ". . . all who listen to me will live in peace, untroubled by fear of harm." Beautiful promises from the Word of God and I believe them and many of you do also; however, sometimes we waiver & begin to lose faith. Yesterday, I asked myself why I begin to doubt when I know I believe. The answer came almost immediately: I feel unworthy. I don't do everything right. I fail from time to time, not necessarily intending to sin, but sinning nevertheless. Probably some of you have felt likewise. The reason we can and should keep the faith is God's Grace, His unmerited favor, Grace is His love to you even though you don't deserve it. Stand on God's promises each and every day and remember He is a God who does not fail. We may, but He doesn't. God bless.

Day 8: Honesty is uprightness. fairness truthfulness, sincerity, freedom from deceit or fraud. I think most everyone admires honesty and want people around who are honest and we can trust. *I must admit that mary years ago, I realized I told little "white" lies for no apparent reason. The realization of this fact made me very sad; I concluded that the habit developed when I was in an abusive relationship where a wrong answer meant I would be the object of wrath/abuse. In order to save myself, I would tell this individual what I knew he/she would want to hear. Lying (dishonesty) invaded other areas of my life. Once I recognized this sinful habit in my life, I set out (with God's help) to change. The Bible says "Lying lips [are] an abomination to the LORD: but they that deal truly/honestly [are] His delight." I encourage you to deal honesty at home, with friends, at the work place, in ALL areas of your life. We do not want to loath, disgust, or shame God with our actions but we want Him to be pleased with us. Have an awesome weekend. God bless.

Day 9: How many lives could be saved if anger/wrath was controlled? How many marriages would succeed if wrath/abuse were not present? The Bible gives us strong advice concerning the sin of wrath. "let every person be quick to hear, slow to speak, slow to anger; for the anger of man does not produce the righteousness of God." - " A fool gives full vent to his spirit, but a wise man quietly holds it back." - "A hot-tempered man/woman stirs up strife. . ." - "Be angry and do not sin; do not let the sun go down on your anger, and give no opportunity to the devil." Your anger in a split second can destroy lives, relationships, and opportunities, "A man of quick temper acts foolishly, and a man of evil devices is hated" Improve the quality of your life and the lives of those around you by eliminating a spirit of strife/anger/wrath in your life. God is here to help you - you only have to ask. God bless.

Day 10: See if you're guilty of one of the following - Are you having marital problems, so you seek advise from your closest divorced friends; you have a drug addiction and you constantly hang around other people with the same problem; you are a shopaholic/deeply in debt and your favorite pastime is to go shopping with other shopaholics. The answer is not to run to the phone with your problems but to fall on your knees before the throne and talk to the One who can 'supply all your needs.' 'Have a little talk with Jesus' First, not after you have exhausted/failed in your attempts to change in your own strength. Most of the time, your friends don't have answers for their own problems, much less yours. Remember - God's Word is Strength and you "can do all things through Christ who strengthens" you. God bless.

Day 11: Several years ago, I had a student in class who stated that he did not believe in God. I asked him privately one time, "Why not?" He answered, "If I choose to believe, I will have to change many things in my life and I don't want to change." Now, I ask you. Do you believe? Why not? Is your answer the same? Is it worth the risk? His answer is most probably the truthful answer of much of our world. We want a life with no rules or regulations or guidelines. But does it bring you peace, joy, happiness, contentment. .? Who do you serve this day? God bless

Day 12: Someday . . . sometime . . . Do you use these words? Have you ever Thought how empty they are? "I'll succeed someday. I'll call sometime. I'll travel someday. I'll apologize sometime. I'll tell them how I feel someday." Someday is an unspecified time in the (distant) future. If we live by those words, we are going to miss out on many awesome moments/relationships. I think it is fear of making a commitment. You cannot depend on spending time with your wife/husband, children, parents someday. Before you know it . . . time will go by - never to be retrieved. How about, do it today or maybe now. Don't waste time with planning to live someday. Even God warns us - "Choose you THIS day whom you will serve." There may not be a someday. God bless.

Day 13: If you have a dream and it lines up with God's Word, it is meant to be. You cannot sit back and wait for it to happen, but you must begin to take steps toward that dream. It will amaze you to see what God can do. On our own we can do little but with God as our partner, we can soar to heights beyond our imagination. In the future we will regret more of what we did not do than what we did do. "The future belongs to those who believe in the beauty of their dreams." ~ Eleanor Roosevelt God bless

Day 14: In this life there is a constant war between the mind of the flesh and the mind of the spirit. Each day we face battles. However, WE decide which one wins in our life. Even as believers we can still operate more in the flesh than in the spirit. We must learn to listen to God's 'still small voice' and follow it with each decision we make. The more we talk with God (prayer) and the more we read His Word, the more we will recognize His Voice and be able to follow God's leading. Practice listening today so you can win all your battles. *An added benefit may be that if you improve your listening skills, you will be able to HEAR your wife, husband, children and friends when they are trying to communicate with you. (haha) God bless.

Day 15: The happiest people are not those who have everything, but they are the ones who make the most out of what they do have. It is not wrong to have possessions, but it is wrong if your possessions have you. To live a contented life and eliminate a lot of the stress in your life, accept what is, let go of what was AND have Faith in what will be! God has told us He will never leave us nor forsake us. He is our provider. Be content - godliness with contentment (satisfaction, peaceful happiness) is great gain. Choose contentment today! God bless

Day 16: Be not deceived; God is not mocked: for whatsoever a man sows, that shall he also reap. Our world is based on sowing and reaping. It is true in the natural and the spiritual. If we would stop to think about what crop we will receive before we sow our words and actions, often we would choose to keep our mouth shut and our actions would be curtailed. One additional principle is that we sow one seed, but we reap much more; sometimes we receive a bumper crop. *If you want to be blessed, bless others; if you need a financial blessing, sow some of your money; if you need encouragement, encourage others; if you need help, help and serve others. Can you even imagine what an awesome world we could have if we would first take care to plant the right seeds. Determine today to plant good seed and watch what God will do in your life. May God's blessings and favor be yours this day and every day.

Day 17: Have you ever uprooted a plant and then left it outside of the pot for several days before getting new potting soil and replanting it? Part of it will have died, and it will take much work to get it healthy and living again. The same with us. "I am the vine; you are the branches. If you remain in me and I in you, you will bear much fruit; apart from me you can do nothing." John 15:5 *If we are Christ followers, we must stay in His presence or we will lose out on the nurturing soil which gives us life. Stay rooted in His Word and honor the Lord. God bless.

SOMETHING DIFFERENT, YET THE SAME

Day 18: How many times in a day do you say, "I'm afraid . . ."? Remember the fear surrounding Y2K? We experience a fear of sickness; fear of death; anxiety over our children, our parents, our finances, our future, fear of identity thief - the list goes on and on. Much of our fear is caused by the hype over a certain situation. Where does this hype come from? the media, movies, print, some 'scare tactic' video games, TV . . . How do we protect ourselves from falling into the Well of Fear? There's only one answer - "Submerge yourself in the Word of God" You will discover that He loves you, will care for you. He knows the end from the beginning and He has promised, "For I know the plans I have for you, plans to prosper you and not to harm you, plans to give you hope and a future." Do NOT fear, only BELIEVE! God bless.

Day 19: If your mind is poisoned with the world and your out-of-control Thoughts, here is the advice given to us in the Bible. "Whatever is true, whatever is noble, whatever is right, whatever is pure, whatever is lovely, whatever is admirable--if anything is excellent or praiseworthy--think about such things." *This takes some effort! When the wrong Thoughts come to your mind, purposely think on one of the above. Remind yourself that God is good, that He is your provider, that he loves you, that you're blessed by your friends, family, job. Think on a great memory (birthday, birth of a child, wedding, trip, etc) Have a great day feeding your mind with 'good' things and God's favor. God bless.

Day 20: Make it a Life-Rule to give your best to whatever passes through your hands. Stamp it with your creativity, your uniqueness - let superiority and excellence be your trademark. *If you do ALL things as if you are doing them unto God, you will never have to worry about doing your best; it Will be your best effort. God bless.

Day 21: I know you have heard it before but it is not easy. ". . . forgive whatever grievances you may have against one another." (Bible) Forgiveness is mandatory if we are to be forgiven for all we have done wrong. For several years, I have not had trouble forgiving others because I realize that God will make things right. Unforgiveness will eat you alive. Just think how much hatred and how many crimes have been committed because of unforgiveness. If I need to forgive someone who has wronged me, I say. "I forgive . . . and I do not hold it against them." I repeat those words every day until I feel the forgiveness. I actually have learned to feel sorry for those who wrong me because I have seen God at work on my behalf. You will live better by day and sleep better by night if you have peace toward others. Forgive - today. You deserve it. God bless.

Day 22: The Bible tells us to "walk by faith and not by sight." Great advice. If we only look at our circumstances, we will become very discouraged. I was just thinking about Christopher Reeves (Superman) who was paralyzed when thrown from a horse. How could anything good come out of such a tragedy? Because of his notoriety, more money came in for medical research. Before he died, there were huge breakthroughs. Who benefited? People all over the world have had better lives because of Christopher Reeves. Do you think his calling in life was to be a super-man in difficult times in order to help the world or to play the role of Superman. I think he was born for such a time as that. Reexamine your circumstances with new eyes. God bless.

Day 24: Jesus taught us to pray, "Our Father, who art in Heaven . . . " If we follow God, we have a Father/child relationship with Him. *What is a father? One who acts in a protective, supportive, and responsible way towards his children. Fathers offer developmentally specific provisions to their sons and daughters throughout the child's life cycle. Active father figures may play a role in reducing behavior and psychological problems in His children. (No matter what kind of biological father we have on earth, we have Almighty God, the God of the Universe, as our Father.) He provides, protects, encourages. He wants us to have peace, joy - an abundant life - more than we can ever ask or think. Start today and every day by repeating, God is my Father. It will make a difference in your view of yourself and your view of God. Have a blessed day!!!!!

Day 25: Many times we look at others and think "they've got it made: great home, salary, their children are successful, etc." However, we have no idea what kind of battles are being waged inside each individual we meet. In fact, everyone is battling something. Don't forget to *Show mercy to all; give kindness in abundance; be a friend to the friendless, extend a smile, a hello, a hug. We are all in this life together. The only way the world can live in harmony is if we let God be our conductor; then, we can create the greatest music ever heard. God bless.

Day 26: "May we not be governed by the flesh but by the dictates of God's spirit living in us." Rom.8:5 We are told that if we operate by the mind of the flesh (with worldly/carnal thoughts) it is death (misery) but if we have the mind of Christ/the Holy Spirit, it is life and peace now and forever. *So, if your life is in turmoil and chaos, stop living by 1st 'Flesh'alonians and 2nd Opinions and turn to the Word of God, our road-map for an awesome future. (inspired by Greg Canada) May God bless you and give you favor today and always.

Day 27: Are you living a life of integrity, excellence? Are you known more for the promises you don't keep or those that you do keep? Do you just let anyone speak into your life? God tells us that we must guard our hearts with all diligence because from it flows the springs of life. Maybe it is time for us to prune some things or individuals out of our lives and to step up our righteousness, honesty, and values. Remember, if you are a God follower, you are to be a living epistle (letter) to be read by man. What is being read by your life today? God bless

Day 28: For sure, there is one thing most people have an excess of and that is an opinion. Most of the time it is an opinion in which we have no investment. It can also be called gossip. The Good Book says: "If anyone considers himself religious and does not keep a tight rein on his tongue, he deceives himself and his religion is worthless." OUCH! But, we are given a great promise: "Whoever would love life and see GOOD days must keep his tongue from evil." *If we throw mud, we get some on ourselves and there's always a stain left on its target. Remember, you will reap the harvest you plant, good or bad. ". . . the power of life and death are in the tongue, and you WILL eat the fruit thereof." Instead of looking at others, try looking in the mirror - then you won't have time to criticize, you'll be too busy working on yourself. God bless.

Day 29: He who gives to the poor will not want . . .Proverbs *Are you a giver or a hoarder? Society has become such hoarders that there is a show featuring Hoarders. I have not heard of one about givers. (I remember one Christmas a family related to me found 2 bags of toys and gifts on their front porch. It was going to be a frugal Christmas until their 'gift' appeared.) What a blessing! In Luke, the Bible tells us that if we are trustworthy and faithful with the little we have, we will be given bigger things. Choose to be a giver today (or increase your giving) and you will not have lack in your life. God bless.

Day 30: There is no pillow so soft as a clear conscience ~ French proverb. Did you know that you have an internal alarm which helps you decide what decision to make? It is called our 'conscience alarm.' When you get that deep down feeling that something just isn't right, it isn't. Listen to that small inner voice; God gives it to us for a purpose. However, sometimes our conscience gets seared. That happens when we know what to do and we don't do it. It's a little indiscretion, nothing major. But many times the minor turns into the major. Make sure your 'conscience alarm' has fresh batteries - recharge daily with the Word of God and prayer; It will then stay in good working order. God bless.

Day 31: Gandhi stated, "If Christians would really live according to the teachings of Christ, all of India would be Christian today." In fact, not just India, but the whole world. Sometimes it is difficult to tell who the believers are except maybe the ones in church. WWJD was a popular acronym, What Would Jesus Do? You still see it occasionally. *Today, ask yourself - Are you an embarrassment or an ambassador to your faith? If we want others to follow Christ, we might want to stop and ask ourselves, on a daily basis, WWJD. The world, including our family and friends, are watching you! God bless.

April

Thoughts for Each Day

Day 1: Most people believe in God. Many believe and go to church. If you ask these people if they have victory, peace, and joy in their lives, you would be surprised at how many 'No's' you would hear. Why? The God of the Universe is all-powerful, but we lack power operating in our lives. It's just like plugging in your hair dryer. Unless, it is plugged in to the power source, it will not operate. Also, there are different levels of power depending on what we choose. *To stay plugged in, on high power, reaping God's best, we must read and meditate on His Word, talk with Him in prayer, let Him lead instead of following us, be thankful, and live a life of service.

Day 2: If you are serving God and following His commandments, you are the head and not the tail, you are above and not beneath. You are blessed going out and coming in. These are God's promises to you. He assures you that you are a Victor, not a victim. You are a champion, not defeated. Don't look to Obama or anyone else to save you!! God can get in your bank account, in your sickness, in your dis-functional family, in every realm of your life and turn your sorry into joy, your loss into gain, your tests into a testimony. Trust God. Walk in Victory. God bless.

Day 3: The Bible tells us to meditate upon God's Word day and night. This does not mean you have to carry a Bible around with you everywhere; however, in the news recently, a bus driver was robbed. When his bus was stopped, the robbers shot him twice. Both bullets hit a pocket-size Bible he carried in his front pocket. Literally, the Book saved his life. *If we will study the Bible, it will transport us into a reality that will transform our lives. We will have peace and joy unspeakable, living each day with an expectation of God's goodness surrounding us. God bless.

Day 4: Last Thanksgiving I took my granddaughter to Barcelona. The morning after our return, her mother heard her crying. When asked what was wrong, she answered, "I'm not in Barcelona." *In life, don't cry because it's over, smile because it happened. ~Seuss. Today, take time to reflect on your life and catch up on your smiles. God bless

Day 5: Darkness cannot drive out darkness, only light can do that. Hate cannot drive out hate, only love can do that-MLK. Peace needs to reign in the world not revenge. If we lived by the rule an eye for an eye and a tooth for a tooth, the world would be both blind and toothless. Live in peace. God bless.

Day 6: Have you ever received this message - "This phone has not been backed up in two weeks. Backups happen when the iPhone is plugged in, locked, and connected to WiFi" Sounds like a message from God? You have not been backed up in AGES. Backups happen when you are plugged in to God, the world is locked out and you are connected to the Holy Spirit. *Don't wait until a backup is needed; stay plugged in, locked out, and connected to live a life of empowerment. God bless!

Day 7: "We make a living by what we get, but we make a life by what we give." ~ Winston Churchill "Not all of us can do great things, but we can do small things with great love." ~ Mother Teresa "The best way to find yourself is to lose yourself in the service of others." ~ Gandhi *Famous people the world over have realized the importance of giving and serving! Have you? If not, get started. If you have discovered this truth, continue. God bless.

Day 8: The Bible speaks of planting seeds, the Word of God, on good ground. Our hearts represent the ground, but is your heart 'good soil?' What do I mean? What you continually plant in your heart on a daily basis determines its goodness; the richness of the soil. Your choices day-by-day (the programs you watch, the people you hang around, the language you speak and listen to, the books you read) dictate the condition of your heart. Remember 'goodness' cannot come from 'wrongness.' Your heart's health determines your future. Keep your heart with great diligence so God's Word can take root and grow. Therein lies your happiness and your success. God bless.

Day 9: When a chapter closes in your life, it gives you the opportunity to go on to the next chapter. Remember that YOU are writing your Book of Life. You are not always in control of what happens but you are in control of how you react to it . . . with every action is a reaction. Many years ago there was a TV show entitled "This Is Your Life." If your story were televised now, would you be happy with the results? If not, get busy, one day at a time to rewrite your story. Have an awesome day - serve others - receive God's blessings with gratefulness.

Day 10: Lay aside the old self, which is corrupted with the lusts of the flesh, be renewed in the spirit of your mind, put on the new self, which is in the likeness of God and has been created in righteousness and holiness of the truth ~ Bible *Don't accept the tale that you are what you are and there's no chance of you being any better, or having any more, or doing any great thing. Get a new mindset. With God's help, rewrite your own story and make it phenomenal God bless.!

Day 11: "Let your light shine before others, so that they may see your good works and give glory to your Father who is in Heaven. ~ Bible *Have you ever thought of yourself as a light into the world? If you give out light, your light does not diminish, but more light makes the world less dark. This is how good prevails instead of evil. "Remember that evil thrives when 'good' men do nothing."-Edmund Burke So, let your LIGHT shine. God bless.

Day 12: For the Lord sees not as man sees: for man looks on the outward appearance, but God looks on the heart. ~ Bible That's so true. Even Shakespeare says "For the apparel oft proclaims the man." People do judge us by how we appear. Definitely not right. Let's try to do it God's way. Forget the piercings, tattoos, too short, too long, too tight, too baggy, crazy hairstyles, and blue finger nail polish. It's more important to be clean in body and in spirit. The next time you open your mouth to criticize, instead, examine YOUR heart. God bless.

Day 13: Set your mind on today and the things you need to do today, take no thought for tomorrow because it will have issues of its own. Don't spend time worrying! 40% of what we worry about, never happens; 30% has already happened so we cannot do anything about them; 22% is beyond our control; only 8% of our worries we can actually do something about. "There are only two things to worry about, either you are healthy or you are sick. If you are healthy, then there is nothing to worry about. But if you are sick there are only two things to worry about, either you will get well or you will die. If you get well, then there is nothing to worry about. But if you die there are only two things to worry about, either you will go to heaven or to hell. If you go to heaven, then there is nothing to worry about. And if you to go hell, you'll be so darn busy shaking hands with friends, you won't have time to worry." Riebe. In other words, put yourself in God's hands; you do your part and He will take care of the rest. God bless.

Day 14: "If winter comes, can spring be far behind?" ~ Shelley *These last few warm days in Tenn. have reminded us that spring is on its way. Likewise, if we are experiencing a 'winter' in our own private lives, remember this too will pass and spring is around the corner. Once, I was in a 'winter period' in my own life, and I was crying my way down Monterey Mountain., I heard God say clearly to my spirit. "If you would keep your eyes on me, you would not be caught up in the storm." I immediately saw, in my mind, the image of God and man from Michelangelo's painting on the ceiling of the Sistine Chapel. Adam's eyes are 'locked' on God's. Keep your focus; God is working on your behalf; your spring is on its way. God bless.

Day 15: Catharsis - a process of releasing and thereby feeling relief from strong, pent-up, repressed emotions. It seems today's world is all about finding relief, a catharsis. They use the media, FB, twitter, email, etc., in order to vent. They take justice into their own hands by expressing fits of emotion on the helpless who happen to be in their presence. STOP! If you need release, a cleansing, go to the

Lord in prayer: "Lead us not into temptation, but deliver us from evil." God has a way of bringing peace and joy to your life. If you must vent, vent to the Master. God bless.

Day 16: Make this declaration today and everyday: Because I honor God in and with my life, He will "do exceedingly abundantly above all that I ask or think." (Eph.) His blessings will chase me down and overtake me. I will be in the right place at the right time. People will go out of their way to be good to me. I am surrounded by God's favor (inspired by Joel Osteen) Expect God's favor today! God bless.

Day 17: If you want to give your spirit a lift today, count all of the blessings you have in life that money cannot buy. You might even thank God for ALL that you have escaped. (Ex. Thank Him for that person you almost married, but didn't.) Take time to rejoice in the Lord's blessings, and look for someone you can bless. May God's favor and blessings be yours, each and every day.

Day 18: What are you feeding in your life? Examine what you give the most attention (time) to. Are you the father standing behind the door, playing with his new electronic toy, telling his little daughter he wasn't ready to play yet that she should count to 1000? Whatever we spent time doing is being fed. If you have a bad habit you want to break, starve it to death by filling your time with something else (maybe even reading the Bible). Don't be like the parent who kept promising his young son they would build a tree house; when his son was hit by a car in front of their home, his son's last words were, "Dad, you won't have to build that tree house now." What controls most of your time? Answer this question and you will discover your priorities. Let God help you get your life on track. God bless.

Day 19: I had a friend who never opened her Bible; she was also a hit or miss church goer. I once asked her to fast for one day, drinking only water/tea and eating bread. She said "ok." I then said, why not fast for two days, maybe even a week. She looked at me in shock, "There's no way I can do without food for that long." My answer, "You go without the 'meat' of God's Word for even longer than that." She got the point. The Bible says to "Watch and pray, that we may not come into temptation. The spirit indeed is willing but the flesh is weak." Bible. We can remain strong in spirit and in our bodies if we feast upon God's Word and pray on a daily basis. Become strong, remain strong with God's daily direction. Have a blessed day.

Day 20: Love is for every day: Sonnet 116 "Let me not to the marriage of true minds Admit impediments. Love is not love Which alters when it alteration finds, Or bends with the remover to remove: O no; it is an ever-fixed mark, That looks on tempests, and is never shaken; It is the star to every wandering bark, (ship) Whose worth's unknown, although his height be taken. Love's not Time's fool, though rosy lips and cheeks Within his bending sickle's compass come; Love alters not with his brief hours and weeks, But bears it out even to the edge of doom. If this be error and upon me proved, I never writ, nor no man ever loved." William Shakespeare *"Love" holds true when she gains 15 pounds and cannot get rid of it when having your child; "love" stays when he has donelap disease (His gut done lapped over his belt); "Love" is constant as the northern star. I absolutely love this sonnet and pray that everyone experiences this kind of love in his/her lifetime. God bless.

Day 21: How many of you are imprisoned by your past or by shame or by bad decisions you have made or may continue to make? I'm here to declare the words of Jesus: ". . .the Lord has sent me to proclaim freedom for the prisoners." If you will let Him, He will open those doors and set you free; our sins (shame, guilt) will be scattered as far as the east is from the west. Tell yourself today, "I am free. No longer will my past nor my present determine my future. It is my choice and I choose to be free." God bless.

Day 22: What is life without "hope"? . . . Hopeless (what an empty word) - Belief in God and His Love for you, gives you hope. "Rejoice and exult in hope, be steadfast and patient in suffering and tribulation, be constant in prayers" - Bible. We have His assurance that He will incline His ear to us and hear us. "Listen to the mustn'ts, child. Listen to the don'ts. Listen to the shouldn'ts, the impossibles, the won'ts. Listen to the never haves, then listen close to me... Anything can happen, child. Anything can be." Shel Silverstein (as long as you have hope and believe In God - put your trust in Him) God bless.

Day 23: Love is the one thing mankind hunts for in life. Many people have a false connotation of love. It is not goose bumps, great sex, or manipulating another to do your bidding. This week, look for love all around you: a child's hand grasping yours, a hug from a friend, a bowl of soup from a neighbor, a stranger mowing/raking your yard, someone going the extra mile to help you attain your dream. As I always told my high school seniors, the percentage of time they will spend 'making love' in a lifetime is minute compared to the rest of time. *Live a life of love; open your eyes to the love you have all around you and equally show love to others. God bless.

Day 24: One day with God is better than a lifetime without Him. God's favor comes upon you. Favor is goodwill, approval, benevolence, kindness, etc. He can open the doors that the world has closed to us. He can provide opportunities that you have only dreamed of. How does that happen? Get in agreement and believe that you have His favor. Dress, act, speak, walk, think like one blessed, like (His favor) is upon you. God's blessings are yours for the taking. He is reaching out for you to take His Hand and believe.

Day 25: From experience, I know I have hurt more over the sorrows of my children and grandchildren than my own. When others do wrong unto them, I am like an animal protecting its young. *However, as parents, a great lesson we can impart is to make them realize that we cannot control the decisions of others, but if we trust God and we are faithful to Him, He has promised to reward us for our faithfulness. Teach them to stand firm at the sign of trouble, press in to Godliness, do their best in the natural and let God do the rest. *They/we are not alone, God is working with them/us. We will overcome and be VICTORIOUS in ALL situations. God bless.

Day 26: "Whoever says to this mountain. 'Be removed and be cast into the sea' and does not doubt in his heart, but believes that those things he says will be done, HE WILL HAVE WHATEVER HE SAYS." Mark 11:23 *What a promise! How many of us are speaking ABOUT our mountains (challenges) in life instead of talking TO them. Don't give up if you don't have instant success, but be persistent, because victory is on its way. I always think of our words as seeds being planted. Good soil (God's Word) but the moment we speak with doubt, we dig that seed UP and it is thrown on a bed of rocks. Keep the faith; mentally, watch that seed take root and grow. Your breakthrough is on its way. God's blessings and favor today and every day.

Day 27: If you want God to work His great power in your life, you need to have faith. The Bible tells us "It is impossible to please God, without faith." It also says "unto every man is given a measure of faith." How does that work? For me, I began trusting God for small things and then it became much easier to trust Him for bigger things when I saw the others manifest themselves in my life. Tell God "I believe, but please help my unbelief." He is there always to help us with any weakness we may have because in our weaknesses, He is made strong. Have Victory today and may His favor be yours. God bless

Day 28: So many times we make a commitment to follow God in our lives; but when we begin our journey, we hop into the driver's seat and expect God to be a passenger. Most assuredly, we are headed toward a minor accident or even a major collision. It's not until we turn the navigating completely over to the One who knows the end from the beginning that we will be on the 'right course.' We need to trust Him with our lives for EACH day's journey. May you have God's favor in your life today! God bless.

Day 29: Trust in the Lord with all your heart, lean not on your own understanding, in all your ways acknowledge Him and He will direct your paths. ~ Bible *God has promised to be faithful if we will trust Him; He has promised to reward those who diligently seek Him. Your day is coming! He will give you favor and your dreams for your life will be realized.

If you will remain faithful in the little things, He has promised to give you even greater things. Rest today in His promises. God bless.

Day 30: God is looking for people to help the needy, to give to the poor, to help the down-trodden, to administer to the fatherless and the widows, to encourage the defeated. Could that person be YOU? We are told, "It is more blessed to give than to receive." I've discovered throughout my life that I am happiest when I reach out and help someone. This does not always mean money; there are many ways to give. I know a man who once gave cantaloupes; it was all he had. He has been richly blessed because of his giving spirit. (This doesn't mean to give to those who won't even try.) I recently returned from Ecuador where an indigenous tribe, the Quichuas, live by a community spirit. If a family is in need, a representative from every other family comes together to meet that need. Isn't that great? Want to be happy? Learn to give and meet the needs of others. God bless.

May

Thoughts for Each Day

Day 1: When no one loses, there are no winners! In our society, we have tried to create a pain-free existence, emotionally and physically. In education, we've been told to GIVE a grade of 50 even if the child did not take the test or turn in the work. Everyone wins! We have created a something for nothing mentality. No wonder, as adults we cannot handle loss, emotional pain, and physical discomforts. We look for a quick-fix: alcohol, drugs, unhealthy relationships. . .*If you need THE quick-fix, THE problem-solver, THE strengthener for ALL our problems, turn to the ONE who knows and loves us like no other - JESUS. He has what it takes to carry you through whatever is going on in your life. Give Him the chance to prove Himself faithful. God bless.

Day 2: Throughout time, many people have asked God how He could stand and allow poverty, sickness, starvation, human trafficking, injustice, child and spousal abuse, etc. As believers, we should know that WE are the answer - God works through each one of us. Ask yourself, "What are you doing to make a difference?" If everyone would do his/her part, the world would be a much better place. Mother Teresa, alone, did her part and what a difference she made. God is waiting for us to step up with our time, our

knowledge, our money, our service. YOU + GOD = CHANGE
*What are you waiting for? God bless!

Day 3: How many times have you heard, "Well, all we can do is pray"? It should be an immediate response - PRAY! not a last resort. The Bible says, "We do not have because we do not ask." Jesus says, "Keep on asking and it will be given you; keep on seeking and you will find; keep on knocking and the door will be opened to you." John Wesley (founder of the Methodist church) was asked how long he prayed each day. He answered, "I never pray more than ten minutes at a time, but I never go more than ten minutes without praying." I encourage you to be in constant communication with God. He is waiting to be included in your day, throughout your day and into the night. God bless.

Day 4: Are you a complainer? Do you realize that complaining is a 'sin.' Complaining means we are not satisfied. The Apostle Paul said, "I have learned to be content in whatever state (situation) I am in." At the time, he was standing in the latrines of a Roman prison. So the next time you start to complain, stop and think. . .Either you will complain and remain or you will rejoice and rise above your situation (J. Meyer). That traffic jam you are in may be the very thing that keeps you from having an accident. Tell God that you want to live a life of gratitude. Thank Him for His many blessings; start with the first breath you breathe this morning. God bless.

Day 5: In life it won't matter how many breaths you take but you will always remember the moments that took your breath away. Holding your baby for the first time; discovering that he/she is the love of your life; visiting a sight you had only dreamed of seeing; God answering a prayer just in time. *Anticipate those moments in life, look for them, revisit them in your memory, for they are the very essence of living. (If you wish, share one of those moments in your journal or in the margins of your Bible). May God's blessings and favor be on your life always.

Day 6: Your life is controlled between your ears; it's your 'Thought life.' Romans 12:2 tells us we are to "let God transform us by changing the way we think." It's like the little engine, "I think I can; I think I can." I used it in teaching. "Of course you can memorize Hamlet's "to be or not to be" speech. *We CAN control our Thought life by not feeding the wrong Thoughts with time and energy. Instead, fill your mind with other Thoughts: Count the blessings in your life, Memorize your favorite scripture, Meditate upon the Word of God: "I CAN do all things through Christ who strengthens me." Start today. May God's favor and blessings be in your life.

Day 7: God cares about our smallest needs. Usually, we do not call on God until it is a major issue. Remember, He is the one who has the hairs on our heads counted. He wants to help us with the most min'ute part of our lives. I talk to God throughout the day. I have a friend who told me that she cannot get God to listen to her because He is too busy getting me a parking place. Don't go to God as a last resort, but seek Him FIRST. His Holy Spirit dwells IN us (if we are believers) and He is ready even before we ask. You and God have a great day today. God bless.

Day 8: "He who is in you is greater than he who is in the world?" This is God's promise for the believer. Through Christ, we have what it takes to be an overcomer, which is the true mark of success. We see the trail leading to the peak of a high mountain. You may think that you do not have the strength to make it to the top, but you will get stronger in Christ Jesus as you climb, and oh what a view once you reach the summit. See yourself as God sees you; do not let nay sayers sap your strength and contaminate your attitude. Instead, Walk in Victory today and every day. God bless.

Day 9: Sometimes we get caught up in comparisons. We live, trying to do what is 'right' in the eyes of God and we barely get by; however, we look around and see the 'wicked' prospering. Such thinking takes away our joy. Never compare! Just remember God's Word - "The Lord laughs at the wicked, for He sees that their own day of defeat is coming." Keep your heart glad because "laughter is a good medicine, it makes for a cheerful countenance." Enjoy life; take no Thought in comparing but trust the Lord in ALL things. God bless.

Day 10: "Be mindful to be a blessing." (Bible) Each of us have the opportunity to purposefully invest into other people's lives. This does not necessarily mean financially; it can be an encouraging word, a smile, an action of love, time - the list is endless. Other people need to see God in your everyday actions. Look for an opportunity each day to reach out and help carry someone's burden. If you do, God will make sure someone will help you with yours. Purpose in your heart to be a blessing each and every day of your lives. God bless.

Day 11: We should not be trying to squeeze God into our very busy schedules; He wants us to fit our schedules around Him. The Bible tells us, "Seek you FIRST the kingdom of God, and ALL other things will be added to you." If you put Him first, you will have the faith in Him to take care of all your needs and wants. "Delight yourself in the Lord, and He WILL give you the desires of your heart." In fact, He will give you "far above what you can ask for or think." I can think pretty big; can you? God bless.

Day 12: if you are living on the edge, there is no room for error. You are a train wreck waiting to happen. If you slip, you will fall hard and fast. Not only will you bring destruction to yourself but to those around you. Boundaries and borders should be adhered to – this means physically and morally. For help in living a safe moral and physical existence, turn to God's Word. He gives specific instructions to lead you to a healthy life. God bless

Day 13: "If we knew our future, most of us would not get out of the bed in the morning" . . . unless we know the One who holds the future in His hands and who gives us the strength to endure and come through troubles and trials. He also gives us the mercy we need to be over-comers and be Victors in the end. Isn't it an exciting thought to know that you know who knows tomorrow and this same 'God' has our best interests in mind? God bless.

Day 14: YOU determine your attitude! Don't blame your actions or your mouth on someone else. Think about this! If you have a flat tire, be thankful you have a car. If your hair just won't do anything today, think about the chemo patient who doesn't have any. When your bills come due, give thanks you have a job. If you are just too tired to do yard work or do your daily jog, think about the soldier who lost legs or arms defending your freedom. And if you are one who has suffered great loss, be thankful you still have an opportunity to make your mark on the world. Take charge of your attitude today and every day. God bless.

Day 15: Selfishness is with us the day we are born. Mine!

Me! My! I want! Our journey in life hopefully takes us to the world of "unselfishness." We MUST learn to put others first or we will never be truly happy. There is nothing more satisfying than to know you have helped someone and made his/her life easier. The Bible says it this way: We must "die to self." This is not easy, but begin today to put others first. Give them the bigger piece of the pie. God bless.

Day 16: We have truly become a nation of pleasure-seekers. You can tell by the purchases we make: TVs (the bigger the better), electronic games, faster cars, boats, trips, music, etc. Now, nothing is wrong with this unless we make it a priority in our lives. The Bible encourages us to walk and live in the Holy Spirit and we will not crave and desire to satisfy the flesh. Be sensible - have BALANCE in your life and live for a higher goal rather than thrill-seeking here on earth. God bless!

Day 17: All of us face temptation! We are tempted to listen to our feelings: as a result, we slip into bad habits, we stay in bed instead of getting up and starting our day. We must be wise and think of what the future results will be if our choices are stagnate. If you falter, don't get down on yourself, just start again. Avoid putting yourself in the path of temptation (change the places you frequent and the people who are risk factors for you). God will help us overcome temptation; so trusting in Him is a sure bet. God bless.

Day 18: Are you living your dream? Are you working toward your dream? "Where there is no vision, the people perish." Bible *Don't tell me you don't have a dream. We all do. God puts it in our hearts. Sometimes we dismiss it, or bury it for whatever reason. Today, dig it up; write it down; move toward the reality of your dream. It will give you direction. Your dream may not come to fruition immediately, but the process will be just as rewarding. God bless.

Day 19: While in the rainforest of Ecuador, I had the opportunity to zip line and do an ropes obstacle course in the canopy of the forest above the Napo River, the largest tributary of the Amazon. The instructor showed me how to use my two safety lines to hook on a steel cable, which would keep me safe if I fell. (I did fall once) Even though my heart beat faster and my hands shook, I still had faith that the safety hooks held me. *Isn't that the same with God? He holds us in the palm of His Mighty Hands and catches us if we fall. We need to trust in Him much more than a man-made cable. Put your trust in Him; have FAITH in the One who can catch us in any circumstances that befall us. God bless.

Day 20: For those that wait upon the Lord shall renew their strength, they will bound up on wings of eagles, they will run and not grow weary; they will walk and not faint. ~ Bible *God has promised to be there in our weakest moments. When we are our weakest, God shows through with His strength. Remember, we are going THROUGH, we are not staying for the long haul. Depend upon God and He will give us the strength to make it through to victory. God bless.

Day 21: "I fear the day that technology will surpass our human interaction. The world will have a generation of idiots."-Albert Einstein. We must never forget that personal relationships are what enriches our lives. And our personal relationship with the God of the Universe will give us credence (faith, reliance, and confidence) toward a blessed future. Trust God, not your electronics. Einstein recognized this and that was a century ago. God bless.

Day 22: The single decision to serve God is not the end but a new beginning. We can then draw closer to Him through prayer, reading the Bible, and associating with other believers. Through time, we'll experience true growth in ourselves. We will discover joy, peace, patience, and self control. We never stop growing; we are raised from one glory to another until we are seated with Jesus at the Throne of God. God bless

Day 23: How many of you are creatures of impatience? More of us are guilty than not. We pray (planting our seed), and we want our harvest immediately. The Bible says "seed - TIME - and harvest." We tend to forget the 'time,' which is undetermined. Some prayers take longer to answer than others. Just like in the natural, some plants such as Bamboo grows much faster than most but the *Puya raimondii* from Bolivia takes 150 years to blossom. Your dream may be on the 'slow' maturation cycle, but the blessing will be even greater. Life operates on this principle and God's harvest is always worth waiting for. Be patient for God's harvest. God bless.

Day 24: Take control of your Thought life. Your Thoughts become your words and your words become your actions, which creates your future. "A Good man brings good things out of the good treasures of his heart. For out of the overflow of the heart the mouth speaks." What are you speaking lately? What seeds are you planting? Do you really want the harvest that is in your future. Remember, you are living out the seeds, which you planted in the past. Plant a better harvest while you still have time. God bless.

Day 25: Ordinary deeds become extraordinary when they are done as a service to others. You may think you are hidden away in no-man's land but God notices and takes account. Every thought, word, or deed is noticed by God. You are not like others, "for your Father knows what your needs are before you do ask them. And when you help meet the needs of others, God makes sure your needs are met. God bless.

Day 26: There is greatness in all of you. "Be not afraid of greatness. Some are born great, some achieve greatness, and others have greatness thrust upon them." Shakespeare "Keep away from people who try to belittle your ambitions. Small people always do that, but the really great make you feel that you, too, can become great." Mark Twain. "Great spirits have always encountered violent opposition from mediocre minds." Einstein. "It is not great men who change the world, but weak men in the hands of a great God." Brother Yun. We are all insured of greatness through God. Live your life discovering that greatness and look for the greatness in others. God bless.

Day 27: Kind words sooth the wounded. They give hope to the hopeless. Words can make or break. Words can inspire and words can destroy. Words have more power than the most powerful bomb. *Have you every thought about your words? Nothing exists but first it was a thought and then it was put in words. Use them wisely. Use words that build; they have great power. They can be a spark, which ignites a dream or they can be a 10 alarm fire which destroys everything in its path. Choose your words carefully. God bless.

Day 28: As we go through our day, do we consciously think about what we say and do? The harsh words we speak or actions we take toward a stranger. Would we do the same to our spouse, our children, or to God? Always remember who could be the receiver of our actions. I was recently at dinner with my brother and his wife. Three months earlier, he became suddenly deaf. His wife has been battling cancer for three years. The young waiter was irritated and speaking very quickly, impatient that they were slow to order. I finally followed him to a area of privacy to remind him he was to serve as best he could. I asked him to look at each person, reminding him that he had no idea what he/she were going through. That's true for everyone we meet. It's not always about number 1 (you). Remember, God never sleeps; He always sees and hears. God bless.

Day 29: We are encouraged in the Bible to run our race to the finish line. But while we are running, we need to ask ourselves if we are in the right race. *At the finish line, will others say, "we lived a life that mattered"? A large funeral was held today for a local fireman who has made a difference. His name is not known throughout the land, but a very large crowd gathered to acknowledge his greatness in the area where he lived. He has created a fire and life safety program in area schools. as well as teaching a healthy and respected view of the men and women who serve the public. You, too, need to live a life that matters; run your race, not someone else's. If you do, you will be blessed and you will be a blessing. God bless.

Day 30: Are you slipping up on your new year's resolutions? It has been five months. Are they now harder to keep? Use prayer as a constant companion to encourage and assist you to meet your goals. If you have the Holy Spirit working on your behalf, you have already won the battle. If you have struggles and trials along the way, God can use them to sharpen you and you will triumph in victory. God bless.

Day 31: We are what we repeatedly do. Excellence, therefore, is not an act but a habit. ~ Aristotle *When making your decisions, decide on your habits for excellence and discard your habits of destruction. Live in excellence and if you cannot do it excellently the first time, then find the time to do it over and get it right. Do you want someone else to give you anything but his/her best? They want the same from you and so does God. God bless.

June

Thoughts for Each Day

Day 1: Each year, you hold the seeds of failure as well as the seeds that have the potential for greatness. You are capable of greatness, but you must plant the right seeds to reap the rewards you are capable of obtaining. It is a daily process! You will make decisions to determine how this day, this week, this year, this decade will end for you. You can either keep moving forward or you will become stagnated and then begin to drift backwards into the very situation you were trying to move away from. Be wise. Let God help. He has promised to give us wisdom, knowledge, and understanding. God's blessings

Day 2: I once read the story of a taxi driver in NY. . . driving down 5th Ave., with a passenger inside, when a big black limo pulled out in front of him. He quickly whipped around the car eliminating a deadly crash. The driver of the limo yelled obscenities but the taxi driver just waved and smiled. When asked how he could respond in such a way, he said, "It was the law of the garbage truck." Individuals take on other people's hatred, anger, and disappointment! If they let it change their behavior, they become a garbage truck."
*FB friends, it is too easy to become a garbage truck - garbage in, garbage out. Don't let the bad attitude of others

affect you. God bless.

Day 3: Please, please, please watch - THE BEAUTY OF MATHEMATICS on youtube.com.

Day 4: Have you ever thought about your range of influence? As parents we know we influence our children, but it goes way beyond that. Each person influences others, and we are influenced by others. Once after school while still in my classroom, a Thought washed over me, "Have I ever influenced my students for the wrong?" I broke down in a floodgate of tears. I prayed I had not led anyone astray. After several days of anguish, God brought peace to my heart by saying, "Yes, Peggy, you have messed up but where you did, I sent others to clean up." It's true, we all mess up, but we need to always remember, people around us remember more of what we do than what we say; however, both are important. Stand on the outside of yourself and judge yourself. If you don't, God will. God's blessings to you.

Day 5: Sometimes we have to make ourselves do what we don't want to do so we can have what we always wanted. Discipline is a MUST in everyone's life. We may not embrace it, but it is a necessity for living the Best life possible. "For the moment all discipline seems painful rather than pleasant, but later it yields the peaceful fruit of righteousness to those who have been trained by it."

Hebrews. *Be disciplined with your life and reap the rewards God has in store for you. God bless.

Day 6: Typically, throughout the year, many of you are thinking about creating a 'new you'. You want to appear at the next corporate meeting or the beginning of the new school year, twenty pounds lighter, or with a chic haircut or color. We examine the package in which we are housed and we want to make changes. We look inside and we want to remodel some of its contents. *Many times, CHANGE seems impossible; we feel overwhelmed! An easy solution - there's not one! But if we invite God into our lives, He will work with us and we WILL be pleased with the outcome. Just let Him take charge as we follow His lead. God bless.

Day 7: While many people are celebrating and are joyful, there are those who are broken, sad, distraught, feeling helpless and without hope. *Where do we fit in? A listening ear, a shoulder to lean on, a hug, a Christ-like figure in the presence of their sorrow. Christ came to give comfort; but we, as Christians, are His ears, voice, shoulder, arms, and feet . . . Go and comfort someone today. In comforting others, you will be comforted and find peace for yourself. God bless.

Day 8: Christ came to bring 'light' into a dark world. The light brought by Jesus's birth needs to live in your heart each and every day of the year, not just on special days of the year. Go forth today and every day with peace, joy, love, kindness, and hope; this will show the people around you what 'light' looks like and others will desire what you have. God bless.

Day 9: Thought for the day: NO WAY!!!!!!! How many times has that thought invaded your thinking. A relationship has gone sour and there's 'no way' it can be salvaged or that you can move on. Your bank account is depleted and your job is in jeopardy and there's 'no way' you can start over at 35, 40, or 50. (The 35 year old was me.) You have received a bad medical report on yourself or a member of your family and there's 'no way' there will be a favorable outcome because everyone says so and they know. Each way you turn and everywhere you look there's 'no way' of escape. Negative situations and faces glare back at you. **Take courage, God has promised there IS a way: "Behold, I will do a new thing, NOW; it shall spring forth; shall ye not know it? I will even make a way in the wilderness, and rivers in the desert." So don't give up all hope but take up the reigns, do what you know to do, and trust God to do the rest. God bless.

Day 10: Thought for the day: In the past I've written about knowing people by their 'fruits'; I've alluded to candidates for office but also ourselves and the 'people' in our world. Some of you out there may not understand what I'm talking about; well here is an explanation. "the fruit of the Spirit is love, joy, peace, forbearance, kindness, goodness, faithfulness, gentleness and self-control." Oh a scale of 1 to 5 how do you measure up? How about those candidates and your friends and family? If we are having difficulties with these goals, the Bible gives us the following suggestion on how to obtain ALL of them: "whatever is true, whatever is noble, whatever is right, whatever is pure, whatever is lovely, whatever is admirable--if anything is excellent or praiseworthy--think about such things." When we control our thought life, we are on our way. A medieval prayer I love says. God "be in my head and in my understanding, my heart and in my thinking, my eyes and in my looking, my ears and in my hearing, may the words of my mouth and the meditations of my heart be acceptable unto you, Oh Lord." God bless.

Day 11: The best gift anyone can possibly give is KINDNESS, and you can give it over and over again; there is a never ending supply. Kindness will be appreciated each time it is received. You, too, are God's gift into the world. Does the world recognize the gift or does it think, where in the blazes did you come from? *Let God's character of giving and love shine forth in you today and every day. God bless.

Day 12: What a wonderful holiday season Christmas is but it should be Christmas all year long. Jesus came to earth so that we may have life and have it more abundantly . . . more peace . . . more joy. *I was just in Charleston, SC and I enjoyed basking in the sun; but as followers of Jesus, we can bask in the Son every day of the year. During every season, let's permit the Son's rays to shine through each of us to show the world His continued love and blessings for all mankind. God bless.

Day 13: Bless those who can give without remembering and receive without forgetting. (inspired by Princess Elizabeth) *When my grandchildren were small, I would get 20 or more 2-dollar bills and they would put them in a Christmas card and write God bless on the inside; we would then go to Walmart, and they would choose people to bless. It was one of the highlights of our Christmas season. What a blessing to both the giver and the receiver. This can be done all during the year because every day is Christmas to the Believer. (Choose you this day someone to bless without expecting something in return. God bless.)

Day 14: The first piece of our spiritual armor used to keep us safe is the 'belt of truth.' A BELT surrounds us, it holds us together just like the truth does. Even exaggeration is a lie. *Liars must have great memories; in fact, lying is just too much trouble. Be a person of truth and integrity. Start today and speak the truth. Without the belt of truth, you may be unexpectantly 'exposed' bringing great shame and embarrassment to you and those who love you. God bless.

Day 15: Greek philosophers, Plato and Aristotle, proclaimed that to achieve happiness one has to perfect oneself in human form. However, a Christian has the breastplate of righteousness (right standing with God) to protect him/her - the second part of one's spiritual armor. It protects the heart and vital organs. Don't let others make you feel insecure or tell you, you are worthless. You may not have arrived at perfection but you are better today than yesterday with God's help. Keep your heart protected. God bless.

Day 16: Are your shoes of choice Ecco, Nike, Crocs, Timberland, Keen, Steve Madden, Chinese Laundry, Naturalizer, Born, Asics? *The third part of our spiritual armor is shoes. The brand name we ALL should wear is the 'shoes of PEACE.' When hell surrounds us; when Satan sets us up to be upset - if we are wearing our shoes of peace, then Satan's plan will have NO power over us. God bless.

Day 17: Our fourth piece of armor is the shield of faith. What should we have faith in? That God will see us through our problems; he will bring us out as champions, as winners, as victors. God is working on your difficult circumstances RIGHT NOW if you are trusting in Him. Our faith shield protects us from whatever weapon is used against us. Remember, "without faith, it is impossible to please God." Just stop today and look at the world around you, at yourself, at your family - yes, there is a God and He loves YOU. Keep the Faith. God bless.

Day 18:: The helmet of salvation is the fifth part of one's spiritual armor. Are you part of God's family? Some of you may not believe in God; however, if we both live our lives and you are correct, I have not lost anything by living my life as a believer. BUT if I am right, what have you and other nonbelievers forfeited by not having salvation, not believing? Everything! Put on the helmet of salvation and remember that you are a beloved child of the most high God and He has a wonderful plan for your life..

Day 19: The last piece of your armor is the sword of the Spirit. That sword is the Word of God. God's Words, straight from His Book, has power to protect us, defend us, and it helps us become overcomers. Pray the Word; be a doer of the Word. *A horse can be controlled by a small bit in its mouth; a ship's direction can be changed by a small rudder; our lives can be changed by our 'tongue.' Our tongues, speaking life, is our sword which will wield success in our lives. Don't forget to don your armor each and every day. Let us be a member of the greatest army of earth. God bless you one and all.

Day 20: Many people cannot move on into their future because they cannot get over what is in their past. God gives us a new beginning each day; it is a gift. However, it is up to us if we take that gift and begin anew. "God says our iniquity (wickedness) and guilt (He) will take away." His mercy is new every day. Know, this day, that you are forgiven. Now, take your first step into a brand new day; you may not be perfect but you are making progress. God bless.

Day 21: Are you guilty of saying some of the following: This is going to be the death of me - You're killing me - I love 'so and so' to death - all I have is bad luck - I hate . . . - I am sick and tired of this or that or someone, etc. The Bible says, "There's life and death in the power of the tongue. Speak life." *Your future is the words from your mouth. Guard your mouth. Ask for God's help in speaking blessings and His favor over your life and the lives of those around you. God bless.

Day 22: Storms come in life; there's no way to know when they are coming or what kind of storm it will be. Some are full blown hurricanes. *What we say and do in the midst of the storm determines how we survive the storm. When Jesus was in the boat with his disciples and the storm came, they had to weather the storm until Jesus brought peace, but they did come out on the other side. The same with our storms; God will take us through if we trust Him; He has promised to work ALL things to our good. He will quiet the tempests in our lives. Trust God in the storm. God bless.

Day 23: When I was in the 6th grade, my parents bought our first TV. It was difficult to decide which great show to watch on one of the three channels. Now, with hundreds of channels, I can only find a handful of programs that I am willing to watch. The Bible tells us, 'Let there be no filthiness (obscenity, indecency), nor foolish and sinful (corrupt) talk, nor coarse jesting, which is not fitting or becoming, but instead, we should be thankful to God and our behavior like God Himself.' *What you let into your spirit is what comes out in the open. God bless.

Day 24: Many of us think we cannot be happy if . . . the people in our lives do not do or act according to what we think best, or our friends or spouse do not buy or take us where we want to go. *Your happiness shouldn't EVER be tied to people or things - your happiness and joy should be from your relationship with Jesus. Let God's WILL be done in your life and your happiness will be overflowing with' joy unspeakable and full of glory.' God bless.

Day 25: Life provides many opportunities, but we have to take the first step. Don't blame missed opportunities on God; you only have yourself to blame. You cannot experience a sunset when it is already dark, and you cannot play with your children when they are already grown. Look for opportunities and be ready to seize the day (carpe diem) with God's blessings.

Day 26: During our busy, hectic daily schedules, do not forget 'love.' That is the 'reason for living.' Jesus- the greatest gift of love, found time to show love during his life on earth. "Be not rude, disrespectful, unmannerly, unbecoming, selfish." Instead, show love, courtesy, kindness, respect toward all, putting on the character of God. *Thanks be to God and His Son, Jesus, for showing us the way to live our lives with the attitude of love. God Bless.

Day 27: Birthdays are not a time to be standing with your hand out ready to receive, but they are a time to reflect and be grateful. When my birthday rolls around, all too often, my heart is filled with awe as I think of my wonderful parents who brought me into their world of 'love.' We had very little financially, but I never knew it. And I'm continually grateful for my family, friends, and the amazing opportunities this 'poor' little country girl has experienced. Thank you, God, for the blessings.

Day 28: Discover the child in you and look for the child in the people you meet. *Everyone of us come into this world with wide-eyed expectations and a spirit of magical belief. Rediscover the magic of childhood by putting on your inner child. The world will once again seem magical and that anything is possible if we will only believe. God bless.

Day 29: For whatever crisis you have in your life or will have in the future, God already has a solution and He will see you

THROUGH it. Many people react to a catastrophic event as if it is the present and the future. If you trust God, you will come out on the other side a victor, a champion, a survivor. You will be stronger than ever before. God bless.

Day 30: What does love look like? I use to tell my granddaughter I loved her but she would just look at me and remain silent. I realized she was trying to understand this thing called 'love.' It is not just words but it is shown through kindness, forgiveness, understanding, acceptance, hugs, kisses - What does your love language look like? God bless.

July

Thoughts for Each Day

Day 1: We are too concerned about make-up for the outer body, and we forget about the beauty of the soul. It needs to be reversed. Practice faith, hope, and love to bring inward beauty, which will show up outwardly for all to see. God bless.

Day 2: Give the best of all gifts - forgiveness. It blesses the giver and the receiver. You will be healthier and happier. The main person who is hurt is YOU when you choose not to forgive. The other person is living his/her life sometimes oblivious that you are upset/angry with them. It really doesn't matter who is in the wrong, make an effort to restore your relationship. Both will be blessed. God bless.

Day 3: Don't let anyone steal your joy this day or any other day. If you are shopping, count it all joy, including the long lines, the heavy traffic and the other disgruntled shoppers. If you lose your peace, you have lost the reason for life itself. I always thought, I have only one life to live and as my dad use to say, "By Jove," I'm going to enjoy it. God bless.

Day 4: Thankfulness begins at home - don't forget to be thankful for the many things you take for granted. "Thank you, Lord, for saving my soul, thank you, Lord, for making me whole, thank you Lord for giving to me thy many blessings so rich and free." Seth and Bessie Sykes. I am sooo thankful for my children, grandchildren, and family as well as my chosen 'family' which includes friends, traveling buddies, students, face book friends, church family and all those I may have forgotten to list. God bless everyone.

Day 5: "There is a magnificent, beautiful, wonderful painting in front of you! It is intricate, detailed, a painstaking labor of (God's) devotion and love! The colors are like no other, they swim and leap, they trickle and embellish! And yet you choose to fixate your eyes on the small fly which has landed on it! Why do you do such a thing?"— C. JoyBell C. *Enjoy the good. Today and always, embrace the colors not the fly. God bless.

Day 6: Don't let circumstances dictate your actions and defeat you before you even try to conquer them. Each day you must make a decision to manage your emotions, don't let your emotions manage you. "Whatever happens, conduct yourselves in a manner worthy of the Gospel of Christ." Phil. God bless.

Day 7: Patience is bitter but the fruit is sweet. ~ Aristotle *Remember, God is never late; He is always on time. However, His timing is not ours. Loose yourself in the moment and live life fully while you wait on God's timing. You will not be sorry. He can make happen what you can only imagine. God bless.

Day 8: We are a society that likes 'BLING.' There's 'bling' on clothing, champagne, cupcakes, cars - we are surrounded by 'bling.' But here's a question for each of you - Is there 'bling' in your heart? Does your heart 'glitter' with the love of God? If so, others will be attracted to the 'bling' in YOU and be drawn to God. You are worth it. The very Son of God died for you. God bless.

Day 9: Ask yourself the following questions: What do you think about the most? What is the first thing on your mind in the morning and the last thing at night? What do you talk about the most? What do you do with your time? The answers will determine what you put first in your life! Do you have your priorities straight or do you need to reshuffle, delete, and add? BTW, where did God end up in your evaluation of self? God bless.

Day 10: "For people will be lovers of self, lovers of money, proud, arrogant, abusive, disobedient to their parents, ungrateful, unholy, heartless, unappeasable, slanderous, without self-control, brutal, not loving good, treacherous, reckless, swollen with conceit, lovers of pleasure rather than lovers of God, having the appearance of godliness, but denying its power." ~ Bible *Does this sound and look familiar. Let YOU not be one of these. God bless.

Day 11: I've heard the story of Sam Walton visiting his stores dressed in his bib overalls checking to see if he was treated differently than other customers who were dressed in business attire. In some cases, it was true. Are we doing the same when we take one look at someone and pass judgment on them? The Bible says, "Judge not that ye be not judged." because if we do, we too will be judged wrongly. Take a metaphorical walk in others' shoes today and leave the judgments to God. God bless.

Day 12: I have a friend named 'Will' and, of course, it is my favorite writer's name. It is an Awesome name. 'Will' shows power, determination, purpose. If we have Willpower, we get things done. Each of us has a choice - I WILL exercise, I WILL eat right, I WILL choose right actions. Our 'WILL power' WILL determine, not only how we live our lives, but it WILL dictate our eternal destiny. Quit making excuses -Take action and use your WILL, not your WON'T, to live your life. God bless.

Day 13: Don't wait until you have everything perfect in your life to be content - it will NEVER happen. Learn, like Paul in the Bible did, to be content in whatever circumstance you are in. *Decide to accept where you are on your way to where you are going. Contentment does not mean giving up on dreams, but it certainly helps you to enjoy life's journey. God bless.

Day 14: Where would we be without hope? H - Heaven, O - opens, P - prayers, E - enter. How awesome it is to take our troubles, our trials, our sorrows to the King of kings and the Lord or lords in His son's name. He listens; He cares. And if we stand on His promises, He WILL take care of us. Jesus is our Mediator, our Intercessor. This day, have hope in God! May Blessings and Favor be yours.

Day 15: Have you ever experienced immobilizing fear? I have! Believe it or not, my friends, but I use to be afraid to fly. I would board the plane with a sick, sinking fear. This went on for years. No one who traveled with me knew - I wouldn't dare tell them. Now, I lay my hand on the plane as I enter and thank God that He will keep us safe. The difference - God's Word: "He has not given us a spirit of fear but of power, love and a sound mind." I say, He's 'God of the land and God of the sea, He's God of the air, He's God everywhere.' Give God your fear today. God bless.

Day 16: Sometimes a door closes with a bang in order to open with a fulfilled dream which you did not think possible. A friend who never thought she could go to college lost her factory job. She then had the opportunity to go to school and she's now a teacher. Another friend was in a horrible car accident, resulting in his change of occupation from business to song writing and performing which became a very lucrative and rewarding career for him. Never underestimate God. He has a plan even when bad things happens. Trust in Him. God bless.

Day 17: "A merry heart doth good like a medicine." Prov.17:22 *When was the last time you had a good belly laugh? Here's my prescription: each day, watch a funny show, read something funny, tell/listen to a wholesome joke (I love Irish jokes and tell them to myself.) I've always loved to laugh. (Research says children laugh approximately 400 times a day; an adult only 3-4 times.) Work on your health today and have a good laugh. God bless.

Day 18: I heard about a man who received a call from his doctor who said, "I have some bad news and some really bad news. The bad news is you have 24 hours to live. The really bad news is I forgot to make this call yesterday." No one is promised the rest of today or tomorrow. Do NOT postpone living today; live each moment you are given. Leave everyone you meet feeling loved, appreciated, and accepted. Speak kindly, hug often, and give compliments and thank you's to those around you. God bless.

Day 19: Time decides who you meet in life, your heart decides who you want in your life, and your BEHAVIOR decides who stays in your life. ~ Ziad K. Abdelnour *Usually, we treat those outside our family better than we treat family. The Bible talks more about taking care of family first and then go outside the home. "Do unto others as you would have them to do unto you." ~ Bible – do NOT do unto others before they do unto you. Examine your treatment of family and others, then adjust. God bless.

Day 20: "Stone walls do not (necessarily) a prison make nor iron bars a cage" Lovelace- many times we are locked into an emotional cage brought on by events/people from our past. *If you have freedom in your relationship with God and in your soul you believe His undeserving forgiveness is yours for your past choices, you can then be released. Ask God to step in and release you from your emotional prison. HE WILL! God bless.

Day 21: After moving from Greece, I lost contact with my friend Philippe who was a student in Paris. I tried to find him to say I had moved to the US, but no luck. I visited Paris a couple of times and tried to look for him in the phone book. After six years, I was walking down the crowded Champs-Elysees at night in the rain with twenty seven people. There was Philippe with his back to me, standing in a long line waiting for a movie ticket. *Don't be discouraged with different situations in life - God can step in and do in a split second what it would take you years to accomplish in your own strength. Talk to God, trust in His Word, and live a life of expectancy. God wants to contribute to all the things in your life. He wants to give you an AHA moment - God bless.

Day 22: I once read about a homeless child who was without shoes; his feet bleeding - a lady walking by saw him and took him by the hand and led him to a nearby shoe store. She washed his feet, put socks on him and bought him a new pair of shoes. While the lady paid, the clerk asked the child who the woman was; he looked up and answered without hesitation, "Mrs. God." *We are never more powerful than when we are God's voice, ears, hands, feet, and resources. If we accept the role of God on earth, our lives will be filled with abundant joy; ALL our needs will be met, and God will bless us immeasurably. God bless.

Day 23: As we grow, we are just dying to get older: old enough to drive, to graduate high school, to drink alcohol legally, to graduate college, to get a good job; we're dying to get married, to have children; dying for our children to be out of diapers, to walk, to go to school, to graduate, to be out on their on; dying to retire - finally, we are actually dying and we have forgotten to live our lives day by day. You cannot hurry the harvest, but you can certainly enjoy the season of growth. Slow down and enjoy the season you are living in. God bless.

Day 24: Raising children is difficult. The media doesn't help. The family dynamics played out on TV and film are disrespectful and usually a shouting match. The Bible gives us some good advice. "Fathers (and mothers) do not provoke your children to anger but bring them up in the discipline and instruction of the Lord." "Do not provoke your children, lest they become discouraged." Loving them is the number one commandment. Real love disciplines. God bless.

Day 25: Your past becomes a quicksand for your future. When you are bogged down by reliving the events of the past in your heart and mind, it leaves little or no room for you to move forward to the joy, love, peace, and victory that is in store for your future. God bless

Day 26: Kindness is powerful. "When we feel love and kindness toward others, it not only makes others feel loved and cared for, but it helps us to develop inner happiness and peace." The 14th Dalai Lama. Kindness is always in vogue. You cannot go wrong by being kind. God bless.

Day 27: When my granddaughter was younger, I showed her old pictures from the early days of Cookeville. As she observed, she looked at me and asked, "was everything black and white back then?" Many people want things to be the same - especially the people in their lives. However, the world is not black and white, it is a pallet of colors - nature and people. Enjoy and embrace the differences! It's a colorful world to be enjoyed and appreciated. God bless.

Day 28: Count your age by friends, not years. Count your life by smiles, not tears."— John Lennon *How well do you measure up? I can honestly say, "I love my life!" I hope and pray that you do also. God bless!

Day 29: How can you be a winner in the game of life if you are not even a player? The game must be played in order for you to win! *Expecting something for nothing will never bring you to the top. I challenge you to begin today to create a life by doing and to leave a legacy for others to follow. God bless.

Day 30: "You must not lose faith in humanity. Humanity is an ocean; if a few drops of the ocean are dirty, the ocean does not become dirty." Gandhi *It's true, the media accents the negative; but we as individuals, MUST accent the positives going on all around us. Today, I saw a traffic jam on my road. That is unheard of. When I got closer, I realized that eight vehicles had stopped in an effort for one lady to retrieve her dog which had gotten loose. You and I have the ability to change 'our world' for the good. Let's watch out for each other and their 'pets.' God bless.

Day 31: Much of your life is decided by the decisions YOU make. 'We can decide how we spend our time, whom we interact with, whom we share our bodies and lives and money and energy with. We can select what we read and eat and study. We can choose how we're going to handle unfortunate circumstances in our lives, whether we see them as curses or opportunities. We can choose our words and the tone of voice in which we speak to others. And most of all, we can choose our Thoughts.' CHOOSE WISELY! inspired by E. Gilbert - God bless.

August

Thoughts for Each Day

Day 1: F.E.A.R. (False Evidence Appearing Real) is the number one reason we don't achieve our dreams. The answer? Do "it" afraid. 90% of what we fear never comes to pass. Fear is turning a weed into a giant oak and its roots are embedded in a poor self image. *Fear Not but step out and be an over-comer. God bless.

Day 2: Whatever you do in life, do it with excellence. Be the best dishwasher, mopper, potato peeler - a few of the jobs George Foreman had before he entered the world of boxing. After losing the Heavyweight Championship of the World title to Muhammad Ali, he came back after 20 years and won the title at the age of 40. How? He believed in himself and he "had God helping him."-GF God bless.

Day 3: Backwards thinking leads to a world of negativity. No one ever makes it if they only look in the rear view mirror and say "if only" or "should've". It is what it is - there's no changing the past. However, you can choose to live today and look forward to the future and see yourself in a world of success. God bless.

Day 4: There are three kinds of people in this world: 1. those that make things happen 2. those who watch things happen and 3. those who wonder, "what happened?"~ Mary Kay Ash Which category do you fall under? Don't be a bystander in your own life! (Gloria Fernandez) God bless.

Day 5: Enjoy today! Even if you are doing household chores or taking care of children - enjoy. This day will pass and you can never retrieve one second. When you graduate, you will want to be back in school; when that child leaves home, you will want to relive one of those 'terrible twos' days. A new car, a house, or a bigger yard has to be taken care of the same as the old one. Will it really make a difference? Enjoy your life - it is the only one you have. God bless.

Day 6: He/she died! Those words bring great sorrow. However, let's look at what comes before. . .He/she lived! Don't you want that for your testimony? You met the challenges of life, and you chose wisely more often than otherwise; you were a great friend, family member, worker, servant of others, employee, boss. Because you lived, others' lives are better. Think upon these words and see how well you will measure up at the end of your life. God bless.

Day 7: Your words are the ARCHITECT of your life. What you say is what you think; what you think is what you believe; what you believe is what you become. Repeat the following: "I have the favor of God on my life; I live a blessed life; I have more than enough so I may bless others; my dreams for my life will come true." *In the Bible, God had to shut a man's mouth so God's will would come true in his life. Your words are powerful. Speak faith not defeat! God bless.

Day 8: Don't worry. (That is scriptural -"be careful for nothing. . . ") Worry is like getting into your car and starting the motor and never putting it into gear - you sit there idling or sometimes you race the motor but at the end of the day, it is all the same - you did not go anywhere. *"In all things with prayer and humility with thanksgiving, make your requests known unto God" He is well able to take care of you and yours. God bless.

Day 9: Dreams change where you are today from where you will be in five years. Dream big. You must begin by stepping out and finding out. Live in the present - do what you Can do - keep focused on the future. God is well able "to do beyond all you can ask or think" but He wants to know if you are serious. It is His wish "to give you the desires of your heart." Now, step up to the plate and hit a home run. God bless.

Day 10: I've encountered beggars at home and abroad, (the poor, crippled, blind, homeless, and tricksters). If I feel a tug in my heart, I give. In fact, I try to keep change in my pocket just for that purpose. I cannot see their hearts, but I know I've been blessed and I am here to be a blessing. Remember, we are God's eyes, ears, hugs, kisses, pocketbooks, and servants on earth. If those we give to misuse the gift, we are not responsible - they are - we are only responsible to do our part. God bless.

Day 11: Loneliness sometimes stems from lack of purpose rather than a lack of people in your life. Loneliness may be "a lack of direction rather than a lack of affection." Look around you and see if there is a need you can fill and "pour your life into it." Take your mind off yourself and let God meet your needs and you meet the needs of others. God bless.

Day 12: You WILL reap what you sow, here and in the hereafter. I have watched this principle at work throughout my life and I know that I know that it's true. I have also observed when wrong actions are planted, it seems a bumper crop is reaped! So, live each day with excellence and make 'right' choices. You will not be sorry. God bless.

Day 13: Why should you let others name you? You are not what THEY say you are! You are more than the color of your skin, your race, your family, your education, your resume, your bank account, your job, your circumstances! If you believe what Jesus did for you on the cross - you are a victor, you are the head and not the tail, you are an overcomer; in fact, you are a prince/princess - a child of the Almighty God. Claim your title! God bless.

Day 14: If we struggle against injustices, wrongs, and adversities, we can take action and be part of the change and we can overcome; however, if we just accept the idea

'It is the way it is,' we heap fuel on the smoldering coals and a fire will eventually burst forth and consume. Be the One who stands up and speaks up for what is right. God bless.

Day 15: The rewards of Procrastination is Nothing. The rewards of hard work, diligence, perseverance, and purposefulness is the realization of your dreams. We hear people say, "I wish I had what so and so has." Question: Are you willing to do what they did to get it? *Get up off your lazy/complacent 'tush' and put your shoulder to the plow and your creativity into action. God bless.

Day 16: Temptation to quit will come. It is inevitable. Sometimes, it will be from people who love us or it appears as self-doubt or society speaking defeat. Ignore it. Disregard! Declare war against passivity. Instead say, "I will not quit. I refuse to give up. My God will see me through to a good end." Refuel your flames! God bless.

Day 17: I once saw a cartoon where a man walked down a sidewalk and fell into a deep hole; he climbed out and the next day walked down the same sidewalk and fell in again; the next day, he was more careful, walking on the edge, but still fell; finally, by the next day, he had learned his lesson. He walked down the other side of the road. Does this describe any of us with destructive habits, behaviors, etc.? If we don't choose to make life altering changes, we will still fall. God will help us walk down another road. God bless.

Day 18: Inscribed on Apollo's temple in Delphi, Greece, is "Nothing in Excess." We, Americans, need to take this philosophy to heart. Excess and greed has brought us to our knees. We're the only society I know that buys, buys, buys and many times our acquisitions end up in a paid storage locker or in a yard sell - sometimes, not even being used. "Nothing in Excess" - "Can you live without it? well, then maybe you should. God bless.

Day 19: "Let us not seek the Republican answer, or the Democratic answer, but the right answer. Let us not seek to fix the blame for the past. Let us accept our own responsibility for the future. ~ JFK *My fellow Americans and FB friends everywhere, let's join together and pray for our own country and for the world. Ask for God to direct us to be the Best Citizen we can be and help us be the answer to the problem not a contributor to the problem. God bless.

Day 20: We can never live peacefully if we are anxious. We listen to others and fear permeates every waking moment; we read the paper or watch the news and foreboding creeps into our thinking; we see the lives of others and nervousness invades our every breath. STOP! The Bible says, "Be anxious for nothing (don't worry) but with prayer, make your requests known unto God." He is the Prince of Peace and His peace will be Yours. God bless.

Day 21: Live a life of expectancy! You never know when God has a blessing in store for you. (Last night a former student bought dinner for myself and another teacher - a blessing - what a Thoughtful young man) Sometimes, people overlook small blessings and just look for the 'big' one. It's the small everyday blessings that punctuate a 'life of blessings.' Go out today and be a blessing and expect a blessing. God bless.

Day 22: Instead of feasting upon what the media tells us what we are not, dine upon what we ARE as children of the most high God. There is nothing going on in our lives or in our country that God cannot fix. Friends, do what we know to do and trust God to do the rest. God bless us and God bless America.

Day 23: "To move closer to your dream . . .remember that when you have exhausted all possibilities - you haven't." ~ J. Maxwell. *You will never see your dreams fulfilled if you fear failure - the motto of success is to keep trying - one step each day. If we do not try, we are our own worst enemy. God bless.

Day 24: Tell your story. No one knows it but you. Share it with your family and friends. Stories connect hearts; they bridge generations; and they contain power when told. Next year put Jonesborough storytelling on your to-do list. You will hear stories that will encourage you, warm your heart, and bring tears of sorrow and tears of joy. God bless.

Day 25: Fame cannot bring light; money cannot bring light;

relationships cannot bring light; drugs and alcohol cannot bring light. Only the Son of God can brighten your life. So each day, bathe in the "Sun -Son". God bless.

Day 26: "Keep your Thoughts positive because your Thoughts become your words. Keep your words positive because your words become your behavior. Keep your behavior positive because your behavior becomes your habits. Keep your habits positive because your habits become your values. Keep your values positive because your values become your destiny." — Mahatma Gandhi. People the world over know the power of thoughts and words. God bless.

Day 27: Live a life of expectancy! If you are living for God and doing the best you can in the 'flesh,' the Bible says God is gazing out of the windows of Heaven, looking for someone with a pure heart whom He can heap upon blessings beyond measure. I met a man yesterday who had bought a chest-of-drawers at a yard sell; and when he got it home, there was $150 taped to the bottom of each of the 4 drawers. His rent was due and he needed that blessing. WOW! What blessing is in store for YOU! God bless.

Day 28: Thought you might enjoy this: "Though we travel the world over to find the beautiful, we must carry it with us or we find it not." Ralph Waldo Emerson. If we can only see the ugly with our inner vision, nothing will ever be beautiful. God bless.

Day 29: To be fully fulfilled in life, you must first fulfill your purpose. How do we discover our purpose? No one can do it for you. You need to have a GPS (a God Positioning System). Discover your purpose by prayer, reading your Bible, and listening to that 'still small voice' speaking to you - you will discover the desires of your heart are God's desire for you if you are tuned in to His GPS. ~ inspired by B. Davis and E. Turner ~ God bless

Day 30: As a society, many of us have become lethargic, lazy, non-committal pleasure-seekers. I use to tell my students, either you will LIVE your life or you will sit back and watch others live theirs. I have some advice in the words of Pastor Eddie Turner, "Rise up and pour your life into something greater than yourself and success will take you by surprise." Give it a try each day of your life. God bless.

Day 31: In life, you will go through the University of Adversity. It is inevitable. It is like mental/emotional weight training. Just as we lift weights to strengthen our bodies, adversity trains and strengthens us mentally and emotionally to become stronger. Our society has reached for a quick fix in a pill or drink to kill the emotions - wrong choice. It is ok to GO THRU. In time, tears WILL wash away the pain and a stronger you WILL emerge. God bless.

September

Thoughts for Each Day

Day 1: Selfishness (pride) is the emotional DNA which destroys. *Relationships are broken, crimes are committed; 'entitlement' becomes the buzz word for getting undeserved and unearned privileges and services. Take account of what motivates your actions. God bless.

Day 2: People were created to be loved. Things were created to be used. The reason why the world is in chaos, is because things are being loved and people are being used. *Ponder upon this! God bless.

Day 3: We are each a priceless work of art in God's gallery. Just like art, there is dark on our canvas, but God helps in adding highlights. He brings us out of the darkness and into the light as we become more Christlike. God bless

Day 4: "I count him braver who overcomes his desires than he who overcomes his enemies; for the hardest victory is the victory over self." Aristotle. If you don't believe this, just talk with one of your friends who is trying to quit smoking or to break another bad habit. But the victory is sweet when it is achieved. God bless.

Day 5: If you are serving the one true God, remember He is greater than your greatest problem. Whatever you are going through, be confident that God will defeat your greatest foe and turn your greatest disappointment into victory. Abide under the shelter of His wing and He will bring it to pass. God bless.

Day 6: Remember, after a storm, new life shows through and a new world emerges. We are never alone in our storm, for God holds our hand and guides us THROUGH. For those not experiencing a storm, be thou the rainbow behind the storm for others.-Lord Byron. God bless.

Day 7: "No matter what a man's past might have been, his future is spotless." JR Rice. Now is the time to embark upon a change. Don't seek to bring the past into your future but seek to make needed changes. God is all about new beginnings. God bless

Day 8: One square inch of skin has 650 sweat glands, 60,000 pigment cells, and more than 1,000 nerve endings - NOW, do you believe in God? God bless

Day 9: "Right is right, even if everyone is against it, and wrong is wrong, even if everyone is for it. " William Penn *If we won't stand for something, we will fall for anything. "Tolerance" does not mean you have to accept that which is wrong. Take a stand. God bless.

Day 10: "Things turn out best for the people who make the best of the way things turn out." John Wooden. It goes along with attitude - Make a decision not to complain and remain where you are, but to press on with what you have been given and do your very best. God bless.

Day 11: When you hear opportunity knocking, you don't have time to play another video game, watch another TV show, nap for another hour, talk another hour or text another 30 minutes on the phone - no, you need to leap up and swing open the door. How many of us let those chances pass us by, even the opportunity to bless someone. God bless.

Day 12: Many people point their fingers at the government, the schools, the Church and expect those institutions to FIX what is wrong with the world. Sorry - it's not going to happen. "YOU must be the change you want to see in the world." It begins with one person at a time. God will always be ready to help if we ask Him. God bless.

Day 13: A fridge, toaster, micro-wave, oven, hair dryer, etc, all have been designed for a specific purpose, but they cannot do anything until they're plugged into their power source. We are much like them! We are designed by Almighty God for His specific purpose, but we will never fill that purpose until we are plugged in to His Power. "There's no power shortage in Heaven. We are powerless but as soon as we plug in to God, power becomes available." God bless.

Day 14: What do you reflect to the world? We cannot reflect what we do not have. What we 'feed' on is what shows. Feed upon God's Word, and His Spirit will be made manifest in your life for the whole world to see. If you feed upon the world, there's no telling what will be revealed. Take great care concerning the 'food' for your spirit man. God bless.

Day 15: As each day goes by in one's life, our Book of Life is filled. I am sure you are like me - there are things in there that I had rather tear out. The Good News is that God will rip them out and scatter them as far as the east is from the west if we ask Him to, and He will forgive us and remember those deeds No more. *What will be written in your book today? God bless.

Day 16: Life begins with an empty page in our "This is Your Life" book. Our parents help write the first few pages but very soon we are on our own. Growing older, we discover there is a divine plan for each of us, but we must discover it. This can be confusing! The answer? The closer we are to God, the easier it is for Him to direct our steps. God bless.

Day 17: The Bible tells us that Christ is the head of the church and we (as Christians) are the body. How healthy is your part of the body? Does it exercise? Does it bare fruit? No matter which part we are, we have a responsibility to do our part so the 'whole' can be 100% effective. How is your part holding up? God bless.

Day 18: No corporation gives full benefits to part time employees, so don't expect a full-time God if you're a part time Christian. (Bobby Davis) *We put God on the back shelf in the corner, reaching for Him whenever we have a need. Friends, It does not work that way! Remember, we have just as much of God in our lives as we WANT. God bless.

Day 19: Death runs in your family, the same as mine. Build your life on that which is eternal, not on the temporal. *We become so secular (worldly) minded . . . wanting, wanting, wanting; instead, we need to be more concerned about our eternal life and not our next purchase, or concert, or vacation. Have a great week. God bless.

Day 20: Throughout life, people get angry at us, we become angry at ourselves about 'stupid' choices we have made, but the most important thing to remember is "God loves us and He is not angry with you or me. He never stops loving us. Rest in God's love and understand that "He rejoices over you with joy and will make no mention of our past sins." Zephaniah 3:17. God bless.

Day 21: Are you unequally yoked with individuals who poison your own existence, your values, even your faith? If you sit close to someone healthy, you will not gain his/her good health; but if you sit closely to someone who is sneezing or coughing, most likely you will 'catch' the sickness also. Take care who you hold close. Make sure their sicknesses (lack of values) does not infect you. God bless.

Day 22: Are you content? We live in a world, which feeds us daily with new products et cetera to entice us to go into debt and to never be satisfied/content. The Bible encourages us to be content (Heb.13:5) If we are discontent, we open our lives to jealousy, envy, hatred, lust ,,, In fact, the more we feed discontentment, the more we are discontent. Practice contentment/satisfaction. "Thank you, God, for all your blessings." God bless.

Day 23: The more concerned you become with things you can't control, the less you will do to improve the things you can control. *Let go of the things you can do nothing about. Let God have control and you get to work on what you know you can do. Doing nothing except worry produces nothing. You do your part and God will do His. God bless.

Day 24: How do you treat your time with God? Is it an afterthought or an emergency contact or is it part of your daily routine? When you are in prayer or reading your Bible, do you take phone calls, let a noise outside take your attention away from your fellowship with the God of the Universe? Would you like it if you are in conversation with someone and all at once he/she just walks away, talks with someone else, or just ignores what you are saying. Many times, this is the way we treat God. We put Him where He is the least disturbance, in the few minutes left at the end of the day, or we make it a quick read instead of waiting to hear what He has to say to us in "a still small (quiet) voice." Schedule your day around God. Put Him in the driver's seat. Do your work unto Him (not that boss who drives you crazy.)You are First in His life, let Him be first in yours. God bless.

Day 25: Don't live your life in Shackles, bound by bad habits, negativity, stinky attitude, envy, selfishness and more; but shake off those hindrances and reach for the stars. If you never try, you will obtain 100% of nothing. If you are living and breathing, You have a responsibility to DO something fantastic with your life. God bless.

Day 26: Never settle for a rhinestone when you can be a diamond. *I want to be the very best Peggy Fragopoulos I can be, and it is a lifelong effort. I challenge you to be a (person of excellence). We all are diamonds-in-the-rough; we must daily let God make the cuts and we can burnish/polish our lives in order to shine while doing God's will. God bless.

Day 27: Are you conducting yourself so others see the character of God living on the inside of you? We cannot do this alone; we need God's spirit living in us to help us, whether we are waiting in line, driving in traffic, speaking with colleagues, instructing our children or whatever the task may be. If we are living for God by lip-service only, we appear as wolves in sheep's clothing. Examine your 'walk' and see how you measure up. God bless.

Day 28: "To live is the rarest thing in the world. Most people just exist and that is all." Oscar Wilde. Is it better to live a short Time and make a difference or To live a long time and nobody knows we were even here? Are you living or existing? God bless

Day 29: It is much easier to be nice and respectful, putting yourself in someone else's shoes and trying to show empathy. Mend broken relationships! Don't let a selfish attitude on your part bring destruction. Always "Do unto others as you would have them to do unto you." God bless.

Day 30: Oscar Wilde observed: "Men marry out of boredom and women out of curiosity, both are disappointed." My parents were married with a commitment for life; they were married for 64 years. Times have changed. Is it society or is it individuals? A Godly marriage is the answer. God bless.

October

Thoughts for Each Day

Day 1: This year thousands of people will die from stubbornness: They will refuse to . . .abide by the speed limit; go to the doctor for a check-up; eat a well balanced diet and limit the quantity eaten; get proper exercise and rest; forgive others; and the list goes on and on. *Are you one of the thousands. We are our own worst enemy. Give up stubbornness and you will obtain a quality life. God bless.

Day 2: "Always do your best, what you plant now, you will harvest later." We have excellence inside but we must make an effort to perform excellently. I ask my students, do you want a "C" doctor, or mechanic, or contractor? No, we want someone working for us who is doing his/her work excellently. Remember, Good enough, never is. God bless.

Day 3: Listen to counsel and receive instruction, that you may be wise in your later days. ~ Prov. 10:20 How many of us would have been better off IF we had only listened to the wise advise given to us by parents, family, and friends. *I saw two young ladies, my former high school students who said - "I did everything you told me not to: I had a child outside of marriage, got married, got a divorce, and I'm now starting to school. It would have been easier to have listened." That goes for ALL of us. God bless.

Day 4: The Bible is God's Word. We cannot give His instructions a thumbs up or a thumbs down for what we agree or disagrees with. For me, it is all or nothing. When you open your Bible to read, let the author open your heart to understand. God bless.

Day 5: I pray you are "inspired to dream of doing more with your life, learn from everything you see and do, care for everyone and everything that crosses your path, and be more than you ever dreamed you could become." (Dolly Parton) From a country girl with great wisdom. Heed her words. God bless

Day 6: We read of leprosy (a flesh-eating disease) in the Bible. Many of us look really good on the outside, but we have leprosy on the inside. Do you have something eating you alive from the inside out? Is it unforgiveness, or anger, or bitterness, or jealousy/envy, or resentment, or doubt, or . . . ? God is your answer - Jesus died on the cross to provide us a cure for ALL our diseases. God bless.

Day 7: The Bible teaches us that the fruits of the spirit are love, joy, peace, patience, kindness, goodness, faithfulness, gentleness and self control. If you want to know which fruits are evident in your life, just take notice to what comes out when someone or something squeezes your fruit. *Ex. waiting in line, being cut off in traffic, spouse forgets anniversary, friend makes you angry. How do you rate? What fruits are you bearing? God bless.

Day 8: Excessive pride brings shame - Remember, 'pride cometh before the fall.' However, humility brings wisdom. A humble attitude keeps pride away from your doorstep and helps us develop a 'right heart' attitude toward others. God bless.

Day 9: Our society is 'Image Conscious.' The Cosmetics industry does not lose money in an economic crisis. Why? Regardless of our finances, we want to look good on the outside: hair coloring, moisturizers, tattoo make-up, ordinary make-up, botox, corrective surgery, liposuction, lip injections; it goes on and on. What would happen if we were 'Heart Conscious? spending as much time and energy on our inner life. This world would change dramatically. Start on yourself today. God bless.

Day 10: If you don't like yourself (love yourself), it will be difficult to love others. I am not saying that you like every thing about yourself; but today, write down three things you like about yourself. Don't live concentrating on just the negative aspects about your personality. Hopefully, we are all growing daily toward becoming better people (Christlike) in our life's journey. This journey does not stop until we die. God bless.

Day 11: Reunions renew friendships and create new

memories. Thank you, God, for our ability to remember. And thank you Pinewood students and my students from Georgia and Monterey for including me in your reunion plans. It's always great fun. I know that many of my readers ignore reunions, even family get togethers, making judgments and conclusions that there's no one you want to see or "I didn't like those people back then, why should I like them now?" Don't miss out on a great blessing because you will not even 'try.' You'll never know what you are missing. God bless.

Day 12: Making sinful choices sabotages your blessings with God in ALL areas of your life. "The Bible will keep you from sin, or sin will keep you from the Bible." Dwight L. Moody. When the protest came up about the posting of the 10 Commandments, I thought, "How ludicrous!" Why would we not want people to live by such wholesome, moral choices? Their disagreement came mainly from the fact that the Commandments were from the Bible. Over the years, many children have missed out on some great life lessons in the name of a personal protest. God bless..

Day 13: Probably most of you are like me - if we are expecting company, especially someone special, we clean more than usual, we want the house to look good, smell good - the lawn manicured. *If Jesus came back today, this moment in time, are we as ready? Is there any cleaning up we need to get done? Would we hide some of our reading material, clean out our closet? Quickly put our Bible on the coffee table? Take inventory today - God bless.

Day 14: I want to be grateful for the little things God does for me. I was mowing my yard today and my phone slipped out of my pocket; but right before I was ready to run over it, my eyes zeroed in to where it lay. Thanks, God. Even though I walk three to five miles daily, I still want a close parking spot when I shop. I seem to be blessed with a special spot every time. I consider it a little God 'wink' for me. Look for the little things in life; it will brighten your day and lift up your spirits. God bless.

Day 15: Oh Lord, lead me, guide me, direct me along life's journey. May my steps be directed by You and may my decisions carry out Your great plan for my life. (may this be my prayer each and every day. God bless.

Day 16: Our covenant (promise) with God is liken unto an umbrella. As long as we are making Godly decisions, we are under the protection of that umbrella; but if we choose sinful, unGodly, selfish decisions, we are outside of the umbrella, therefore, out from under God's protection. Take care less you lose God's protection for yourself and your family. This can happen without you noticing it. God bless.

Day 17: No matter how hard we try to make things happen the way we want them to, there is no guarantee. The guarantee we do have is trusting God with our lives. He can do a much better job helping us make decisions, guiding us, and making things happen for us. God's power, not ours alone, is the key to a wonderful future. God bless.

Day 18: What forces shapes you? Examine yourself and ask this question. Is it your family, your friends, the media, the government, your faith? You may need to prune some of the negative influences out of your life or turn to other sources for more positive guidance. The world is full of inspirational books, motivational programming, not to mention you can sit down with the Bible, written by the one and only God of the Universe. God bless.

Day 19: Prayer is a conversation with God. You don't have to sound spiritual nor is there any formula - you need only to thank Him for all your blessings, petition Him for the needs in your life, pray in Jesus's name, then listen for Him to speak to your spirit. If you need guidance, check out the Lord's Prayer. It was a model prayer prayed by Jesus Himself. God bless.

Day 20: When John Wesley was asked how long he prayed each day, he replied, "I never pray more than 10 minutes, but I never go more than 10 minutes without praying." *God doesn't care about the length or eloquence of our prayers, He, like any Father, wants to hear from His children. Don't neglect to talk to your Father each and every day, not just when you want something. God bless.

Day 21: Do you think there is a possibility there could be another Shakespeare, a Michelangelo, a Dante, an Edison, a Thomas Jefferson, or other greats alive today? Definitely! They could be living dormant somewhere. But because of their lazy, lethargic, apathetic, unwilling attitudes to do their very best or to do anything at all, they will not live out their true God given purpose in life. Could that someone be YOU? God bless.

Day 22: Your life will be as big as the dreams you dream! Begin with a thought that is deep down inside your spirit man/woman, take action on that 'thought ', and move toward making your dream a reality. Many adults talk themselves out of the possibility of fulfilling their innermost purpose in life. Success IS in your future if you don't give up before you even begin. God bless.

Day 23: The tomb was empty and still is. However, He, Jesus, lives and He can live in your heart today, bringing you an abundant and a fulfilled life of joy and peace. The only thing you have to do is "Believe." God bless.

Day 24: You may be the very one someone needs in his/her time of crisis - a shoulder to lean on, a prayer partner, a friend - you can be the rainbow behind his/her cloud. Don't miss an opportunity to be a blessing. Mark Twain said that humor and getting someone to laugh is a blessing. Isn't that the truth.? During a smile or a laugh, you can forget your problems, just for that moment in time. God bless.

Day 25: Do you live a life of indulgence? Do you give in to every desire? Are you spending tomorrow's prosperity today? STOP! Take account and make needed changes. Self control is the answer to life-long happiness and prosperity. God bless.

Day 26: Do you play the comparison game? Make a decision today to never compare yourself to others again. (And don't compare your children with each other or with other children. Each one of us is uniquely and wonderfully made. God knew what we were before we knew ourselves and He loves us and accepts us and helps us to be all He has designed us to be if we will allow Him to. Since we are unique, distinctive, one of a kind, there is NO WAY we compare to anyone else. God doesn't compare, so why should we? God bless.

Day 27: Some people have made the comment, "It must be nice to live in "Peggy's World." They think I've never had a problem. If they could look through the window of the past, they would see I had a less-than-good marriage, polio as a child, cancer as an adult, difficult work situations, started over at 35, single parent of two children and more. But, I have always chosen to be HAPPY. It is your choice too. A negative person never sees happiness. "This is the day that the Lord has made; I will rejoice and be glad. God bless.

Day 28: Are you stuck in a rut? Is your Hope-a-meter registering closer to 0 than 10? Are you living on Deadend Street? Without Hope, we cannot even inspire ourselves. *Begin each day with a Belief and a Hope and an expectancy that the Best is yet to come. If you do, your Hope-a-Meter will overflow and you will believe that anything is possible. (inspired by B. Cox) God bless.

Day 29: Do you ever feel a quickening in your spirit to stop doing something you've always done, or to stop saying something you have always said, or to stop hanging out with someone you know has a negative influence on you? That is a nudge from God, wanting you to hone, sharpen your spirit man which will enable you to rise to a higher level so God may bless you abundantly. Listen to that 'still small voice.' God has an awesome blessing in store for YOU. God bless.

Day 30: Get your mind off yourself! "Let each one of us make it a practice to please (make happy) his neighbor for his good and his true welfare, to edify him (to strengthen him and build him up." Rom. 15:2 When we help others, it is food for the soul which strengthens us in return. If we share physical food with others, both are fed in the natural; however, in the spirit realm, if we feed others to lift them up and fortify them, we are 'fed' even more than they are. God bless.

SOMETHING DIFFERENT, YET THE SAME

Day 31: Do you know someone who whines about everything? Maybe it is not a full-fledged complaining but just a little BMW (bitch, moan, and whine) * Perhaps that someone is YOU. I am here to tell you that you will never be happy in life and you will never be a WINNER if you don't stop whining. Try it today. Look at the positive. God bless.

November

Thoughts for Each Day

Day 1: Love covers a multitude of sins - it does not proclaim them from the rooftops - in fact, it does the opposite. If you forgive the person who has wronged you, and cover (don't tell) what he/she did to you, it gives you power. If you tell everyone and do not forgive, it destroys YOU. "Get rid of all bitterness, rage and anger, brawling and slander, along with every form of malice. Be kind and compassionate to one another, forgiving each other, just as in Christ God forgave you. *Clean out your closet of unforgiveness and nail the door SHUT permanently. God bless.

Day 2: Are you living a 'legacy?' No, I am not talking about money; I am talking about good character, honesty, values, and a moral life. This kind of legacy will help your relatives and friends more than a monetary legacy. Your port folio may be prestigious but not as respected as an moral legacy. Someone is always watching your choices; choose wisely so that your legacy in life will point others in the right direction. God bless.

Day 3: Do you want excellence out of others? the person who cuts and styles your hair, does your nails, cleans your house, cuts your lawn, cooks and serves your food, repairs your car – even your doctor, dentist, pilot. Of course, we think we deserve excellence. How excellent are YOU? Do you strive to live a life of excellence? The Bible teaches us we will reap what we sow. Let excellence be your goal and you will discover the excellence in others. God bless.

Day 4: "Perhaps travel cannot prevent bigotry, but by demonstrating that all peoples cry, laugh, eat, worry, and die, it can introduce the idea that if we try and understand each other, we may even become friends." ~ Maya Angelou *This quote demonstrates what I love most about travel - we (humankind) are all the same - Shakespeare said, "If you do cut us, do we not bleed?" I have friends on all continents (except Antarctica) because of travel. I've embraced our similarities and built bridges of understanding of our differences. There have been great rewards and my life is enriched. God bless.

Day 5: "Stinkin' Thinkin'" can steal your joy, take away your hopes and dreams, destroy your relationships, and ambush your faith. Remember, you are what you think. You become what you meditate upon. *Each morning, examine yourself from the neck up. Take time to clean up your 'Thought' life before starting your day. God bless.

Day 6: Worry is NOT from God. In Matt. 6:30, He says, "Do not worry or be anxious." It is easy to entertain such thoughts: 'will my family be ok?' 'will I pass the test? 'will I ever get married?' 'will I get that promotion/job?' 'will the money be there for me to go to school?' The questions go on and on. When you begin to feel anxiety, say – "God will take care of me - He takes care of the birds in the air and the flowers in the field; I know He is on my side and He loves me and He WILL take care of my needs. God bless.

Day 7: When your mind says, "Give up," and your friends, family, and the world agrees, God is the One, deep down in your 'spirit man,' who says, "Try it one more time." The God of Hope WILL see your dreams come true. If it is God's will for your life, no one nor nothing will keep you from success. *Thomas Edison said it took him over 1000 steps to make the light bulb - he did not count them as 1000 failures. Just get up each morning and say, "Today, I will do at least one thing toward making my dream a reality." God bless.

Day 8: Nuggets of gold. Each one of us has a nugget unlike anyone else. Life gives us the opportunity to discover our nugget (gift) and then to use it for God's Will to be done in our lives. Sometimes that discovery will surprise us. *One gentleman at the WBHS Class of '73 reunion told me 'thanks' for allowing him to graduate with a D- in senior English. His plan had been to go into science with an A in Physics but the low English grade changed his path. God had other plans - he is a minister of the Gospel and just recently published a book. God is full of surprises! That's one of the fun things about life. There's always surprises. God bless.

Day 9: How can one not believe in God? Some people put more faith in a 'big bang' theory - Really? Would you believe that there was an explosion in a factory and a car was the result. No way. The Universe is too precise to have just happened. The human body amazes me: organs, enzymes, hormones, cells, DNA. I believe in the great Designer - God the Father, Maker of Heaven and Earth, of Everything visible and invisible. You should too. God bless.

Day 10: Sometimes we become bogged down by concentrating on our enemies instead of living out God's Will in our lives. In Deut. 33:27 the Bible says, "The eternal God is your dwelling-place, And underneath are His everlasting arms. And He WILL thrust out your enemy from before you, and Destroy." *I actually feel sorry for those people who come against me because they don't have to worry about little ole me, but they do have to worry about a big God. Almighty God is my Avenger and He can be yours too if you will put your faith in Him. God bless.

Day 11: Are you sick and tired of being sick and tired? Make a decision today to get an attitude adjustment. How do you do that? Open the Bible and read the Word of God. See for yourself what He has in store for you. Place your hopes and dreams on the God of Hope, and you will realize that you are no longer 'sick and tired' but you have 'faith and hope' for a good future for yourself and your family. God bless.

Day 12: One of the toughest things to do is to take that first step to begin (anything); but the next pit you can fall in to is to become discouraged and stop in the middle and never finish. I've been trying to get this devotion book published for months. It seemed that everything came against me. At one time my oldest sister had fallen and 8 staples were in her head, my other sister suffered a stroke and was in the nursing home and my brother was having heart surgery. I was ready to give up. I just didn't have the time. However, I reminded myself of my own words. Please be encouraged; God wants to see you (me) through to the very end and we WILL finish with His support. Find strength to continue in the Lord. God bless.

Day 13: Do you live your life by taking 'guilt' trips? you stay at 'last resort' hotels? you attend 'pity' parties? and you hang out with the 'Done' family - should have Done, would have Done, and could have Done. Know them? Remember - your past mistakes do NOT have to hold you back. Bible - "For I will be merciful and gracious toward their sins and I will remember their deeds of unrighteousness NO more." Don't let your past mistakes hold you back. You are forgiven. (inspired by J. Meyer) God bless.

Day 14: What kind of person is your 'inner man?' Do you pretend to be one kind of person on the outside and live a secret life on the inside? Society would like you to believe that what you do in secret does not affect your professional life, family life, and moral decisions. - That's a LIE! It does matter! The Bible tells us, "what is done in secret will be proclaimed from the mountain tops." Make changes today - clean out your 'inner man' closet. God bless.

Day 15: Is fear holding you back? Do you fear the future? Do you experience a foreboding about decisions you need to make? Fear is number one in keeping us out of the perfect will of God. Make a decision to "do it afraid." Don't let fear keep you from experiencing God's best in your life. Throughout the Bible, we are told. 'Do not fear.' 'Don't be afraid.' (I use to be afraid of a lot of things. My parents were over protective because I almost died at 18 months. I could never do a somersault; however, with my heart in my throat, I finished a ropes course which had three zip lines. It was located high in the canopy of the rainforest along the Amazon River in Ecuador. My God is the God of the air, He is God everywhere, and He can keep me safe on the ground or when I'm trying to conquer the challenges of a ropes course at the age of 65. God bless.

Day 16: What do you do with your time? We know all the expressions: save time, time flies, on time, in the nick of time, time is money, more time. Most importantly, we must remember that time waits for no man and we cannot turn back time, for only time will tell what we as individuals have done with the time allotted to us while here on earth before our time runs out. Because our time here will determine how we will spend 'eternity' where time is not kept and there are no clocks. God bless.

Day 17: There's nothing like HOME! I'm home: I've seen family, talked with friends, washed clothes, made appointments, worked out: back to a routine and it feels good. Thank you, God, for the blessing of traveling with my oldest grandson and his best friend to Greece and then touring with relatives, friends, and former students on their first Greek adventure. In addition, I visited my Greek relatives, former students and friends; this Greek Odyssey was a memory of a lifetime. *Learning to appreciate all aspects of life makes life, whether home or abroad, an adventure. Thanks to God for providing me with all these opportunities. God bless.

Day 18: The more you talk about your problems, the more your joy will decrease. Concentrate on speaking about the good in your life and your joy and peace will increase. Whatever you speak will be magnified. Make wise choices with your words -inspired by J. Meyer. God bless

Day 19: The best way to solve your problems is to face them. Don't ignore them; don't pretend they don't exist. They will hide in wait and then raise their ugly heads when you are alone with your thoughts. They definitely won't go away. Ask for God's help in solving those problems and take the first step in doing what you CAN do and let God do the rest. God bless.

Day 20: And God said, "It is good!" The beauty of this earth is a gift from God. While gazing on the crystal blue seas of the Mediterranean, I am reminded that We each must do our part to take care of God's gift. Inspired by my friend

Helen *God bless.

Day 21: When one chapter of your life closes, another one opens. Look forward to what God has in store for you. Don't try to re-read the former chapters. Don't concentrate on the medals you've won in the past, look forward to the medals you can win in your future. The awards may be in different areas but their significance is just as important. Look forward with arms wide open to embrace your future. God bless.

Day 22: As I have traveled throughout Greece, I have noticed the Greek flag flying everywhere. Stores, historic sites, homes, streets, the beach, hotels, You cannot go a block without seeing the blue and white flag. I would like to see the same thing happen in America. Teach our children patriotism and love for their country. Let's fly our red, white, and blue ALL year not just on holidays. God bless the USA!

Day 23: When traveling, one is introduced to the history and creations of the past generations who paved our modern day life. I wonder what future generations will say about what we have left behind as our legacy. - inspired by Ginny Tayes. God bless.

Day 24: The moment we take our first breath, two things begin to happen. We begin to live and we also begin to die. Keep both in mind, always. Don't concentrate so much on one that you forget the other. When you make your decisions in life, decide with these two certainties in mind. Live a life so that you can die with few regrets. God bless.

Day 25: In this wonderful holiday season, make sure your behavior is filled with thanks and much of giving. After watching the madness of Black Friday, it was evident that 'humanity has turned Thanksgiving into shopping lunacy and Christmas into insanity.' You can be the one who reminds others the 'Reason for celebrating these two Seasons.' God bless. (inspired by Bobby Davis)

Day 26: "Check the records. There has never been an undisciplined person who was a champion. Regardless of the field of endeavor, you'll find this to be true." Zig Ziglar Don't think you can go through life and just accidently wind up on top when you sleep til noon, watch TV or play games until midnight and live on part time jobs or a government check and become independently wealthy or a star athlete. It just won't happen. Champions have strict schedules; their lives are planned, and they adhere to their plan. In the end, it is all worth it, but you will never find out until you try. I remember one of my students was recognized at graduation for never missing a day of school in 13 years (HB). That's discipline! and good health. Put discipline in your life and reap the rewards. God bless.

Day 27: Some people want to keep God locked in a box,

taking Him out whenever He is needed. It just doesn't work that way. You cannot expect Him to show up on command. He wants to be with you 24/7. He is interested in your everyday life. He wants to be included in all that you do. If you look at God's presence as ever present, it helps you make 'right' decisions on a daily basis. Take Him out of the box and keep Him riding on your shoulder, whispering in your ear, helping you make each and every decision. God bless.

Day 28: There's nothing more fulfilling than to know you are loved by God Almighty. God created love, and He is our example for showing love to others. The Bible states, "God is Love." If you are loving on someone because you are expecting something from the action, it is not love at all. Put God's unconditional love into practice. The more you do, the more natural it will become. God bless.

Day 29: On Mars Hill in Athens, Greece, Paul stood and taught the Athenians about the "unknown" God and His son Jesus. What god do you have in your life that needs to be replaced with the one true God and His Son Jesus? Money? Sex? Hobbies? Sports? Examine your heart and ask yourself what god are you teaching to those who are in your life? God bless.

Day 30: Enjoy life's 'little treasures,' because we don't know when they will be taken away. What am I talking about?

Perhaps, your vision, hearing, the ability to walk, talk, remember. The same goes for the friendships you have, the freedoms you enjoy, and the daily blessings you receive. Thanks, readers, for giving me the opportunity to impart my daily thoughts into your lives. God bless.

December

Thoughts for Each Day

Day 1: God's beauty is all around - with the landscape you see, the people you meet, the God inspired creations of man. May we never take His beauty for granted. "But ask the animals, and they will teach you, or the birds in the sky, and they will tell you; or speak to the earth, and it will show you, or let the fish in the sea inform you. Which of all these does not know that the hand of the LORD has done this? In his hand is the life of every creature and the breath of all mankind. "I thank God daily for the life I am living and the opportunities I have had. Be grateful and be blessed. God bless.

Day 2: If you only trust your own intellect or talents as a basis of your confidence, you have reason to fear but if your confidence is in God you have nothing to fear. - Daily Devotion. "For the LORD will be your confidence and will keep your foot from being caught." Turn your fear over to God. Be confident that He will see you through to a good end. God bless.

Day 3: How do we know God's Will for our lives? The answer: we must pray and seek His guidance. If we are operating in God's will, we will feel at peace. It brings us confidence. Helen Keller said, "Optimism is the faith that leads to achievement. Nothing can be done without hope and confidence." **Nothing done outside of His Will will ever prosper and bring us joy and peace like God can bring. God bless**

Day 4: In the midst of difficulties and hardships come amazing opportunities. Many times life's challenges act as graves, and we feel buried with no hope for a resurrection. We must learn to rise above conflict, suffering, poverty, and need. Use these difficulties as stepping stones to continue toward your destiny. Keep your eyes open to the possibilities. Never give up hope. You are never alone; God is always on your side. God bless.

Day 5: Genius doesn't get the job done. It takes effort, hard work, determination, and diligence. *Just think about all of the brilliance that lies dormant because these qualities are ignored. We All may not be a genius, but we have the ability to do our best if we will make the decision to do so. The Wright brothers were bicycles makers, and they had no formal education; but by watching birds in flight and much study, they were the first to fly. I thank God for the Wright brothers; because of them, I have been able to travel to six continents. God bless.

Day 6: If you nurture your body, your mind, and your spirit, you will gain a new perspective about life. You will feel stronger, your thoughts will be positive, and your spirit will believe you can do anything. If you ignore a physical problem, such as diabetes, and you don't properly care for it, the result can be catastrophic. The physical can affect the spiritual and mental; likewise, the mental and spiritual has a direct correlation with the physical. The right perspective and balance adds years to your life and peace to your soul. God bless.

Day 7: Change takes place immediately. It is the time one takes to make a decision that takes a long time. You may be indecisive, going back and forth. Once the decision is made, change begins. Quit straddling the fence. Revisit your decision each day and do at least one thing to carry out the change you want made in your life. God bless

Day 8: My life – "my personality, my habits, even my speech is a sum total of the books I choose to read, the people I choose to let in my life, and the thoughts I choose to tolerate in my mind." - Andy Andrews. *it is also the same for you. It's all about choices. Whatever we are living now has been built on our past choices. Choose today what you want your future to look like in five years. God bless.

Day 9: People the world over, whatever race or religious conviction, rich or poor, educated or not, love their children, want the best for them, and would sacrifice their own lives for them. Loving our own children defines love for us. I use to tell my teenage students that the reason they were born babies was so their parents would learn to love this cuddly, cute, look alike of theirs before they reached their teenage years and became unbearable. However, our feelings for them are the same through good and through difficult times. That is called Love, unconditional love. If that's not the case with you, it should be. We should not love based on what others can do for us and what is convenient for us but love without purpose other than God told us to "love our neighbor as ourselves." God bless.

Day 10: While standing on Mars Hil, I realized how alone Paul must have felt when talking to the Athenian pagans about the "unknown God". Sometimes, we feel all alone standing for what is right as we go up against society's wrongful choices; however, we too are like Paul. Standing with Paul and standing with us is God Almighty and His son, Jesus. Just don't be afraid to stand. God bless.

Day 11: Pride does not allow for failure. If you are prideful, failure will be devastating; if you see life as a work in progress, then failure can be viewed as a learning process to improve your decisions and actions. Too much pride can take the joy out of life. I've heard it said that "failure if the first step toward victory. InTouch. Leave excessive pride behind and work toward the goal. God bless.

Day 12: Each day someone is keeping count, someone is looking, someone is recording our words, our deeds, our attitudes. That someone is GOD. Yes, we will slip, but He looks at our hearts to see if we are doing our best. It is just as important what we do at home behind closed doors as what we do In the open. We can not hide from God. "For whatever is hidden is meant to be disclosed, and whatever is concealed is meant to be brought out into the open." Have a God kind of day and God bless.

Day 13: As you head to work today, remember you are not what you do. You are a child of God Himself, maker of the universe. Do your work today by thinking that Jesus is your supervisor and God writes your paycheck. Remember, your 'who' and your 'do' are not the same. Your 'who' as a believer is that you are one of God's children and your 'do' is your occupation. My 'do' is to teach but I am much more than that and so are you. God bless.

Day 14: Your attitude is catching. Embrace the good in your life and rejoice. What satan (I refuse to capitalize his name) plans for your destruction, God will turn it around for your good. Remember this and keep a good attitude for yourself and for all those you come in contact with. Bad attitudes provide a way for satan to invade your life. Keep him out by developing a Godly (Christlike) attitude. God bless.

Day 15: Don't try to run away from your problems because you cannot. They will catch up with you, meanwhile, they have grown bigger and become more foreboding as time passes. Face them head on. Do not ignore them but deal with them one step at a time. God will help guide you through. What started as a mountain, becomes a hill, becomes a boulder, becomes gravel and finally sand and you can just brush it away.God bless

Day 16: If you are me-centered, you will never find total contentment and happiness. You will always want more and you will wear yourself out trying to get it. Become Christ-centered. "For through Christ all things are possible." God bless.

Day 17: Do you want more In your life? More prosperity, more victory, more guidance, more confidence? Spend more time with God. He is your friend, your confidant, your advisor, your partner - He will be whatever you need. More of Him means more of everything. God bless!

Day 18: Learn to manage your emotions or they will manage you, controlling your life. Emotions are fickled and they cannot be trusted. Negative emotions such as anger, worry, anxiety, resentment, bitterness, fear, and unforgiveness create unhealthy mental and physical health. The healthier our emotions are, the healthier and happier will be our lives. God created emotions; therefore, God will help you in this endeavor. God bless.

Day 19: The people perish for a lack of vision. ~ Bible
*Where are you headed? Do you have a vision for your life? If not, where will you end up? Lost? Confused?

Disillusioned? Dissatisfied? Unfulfilled? Sit down with God and see what He has placed on your heart and write down your vision (your life's goals). Then begin today to pursue what is in your heart, taking one step at a time to reach your destination. God bless.

Day 20: "Teach us to number our days that we may get a heart of wisdom." (Psalm) When we are young, we think we will live forever; however, as the years pass by and our children grow up (seems like overnight), we realize that we just might have less life left than we had before, meaning we have already lived most of our lives. This can be a sobering thought. What have you done with your life? Have you make wise decisions? Have you lived your dream? Have you worked on your Bucket List? or have you just existed from day to day, thinking you have plenty of time? If we will contemplate life and know that our days are numbered, we will get busy living and not waste one minute. We will be much wiser as we live each day because we have no idea if this day will be our last. Mend relationships, love on family and friends, and draw closer to the Lord in whatever number of days you have left. God bless.

Day 21: The saddest aspect of life right now is that science gathers knowledge faster than society gathers wisdom."- Isaac Asimov *Take the time to think wisely and make wise decisions in order to live a life of quality and not one of regret. There are many things more important than a fast paced life in which you have to scrambled to catch up. God bless.

Day 22: "Holding onto something that is good for you now may be the very reason why you don't have something better." ~ C. JoyBell C.*You may be content to splash around in the puddle you are in but you will never enjoy the opportunities of the ocean or the sea unless you are willing to take a chance and make a change in your life. God bless.

Day 23: We need 'down time' in our busy lives. Take time to just 'be.' Rest and refresh. Sip your coffee, talk with a friend, read a good book, smell the roses - carpe diem. "Rest is not idleness, and to lie sometimes on the grass under trees on a summer's day, listening to the murmur of the water, or watching the clouds float across the sky, is by no means a waste of time. John Lubbock. Every life needs balance. God bless.

Day 24: Lessons in life - when we know better, we do better; to love someone is to liberate, not possess them; negative words have the power to seep into the furniture and into our skin; we should be grateful even for our trials. ~ Oprah *Have a blessed day . . . do your best, love like you want to be loved, speak positive over your life and the lives of others and your negatives will become positives. God bless.

Day 25: The tears we shed are a testament to the love we have for those individuals who have touched our lives. Never regret those tears but remember them as a monument for having loved. God bless.

Day 26: Americans are all about brand names. Whether you wear Nike, Guess, J Crew, Gap, or Forever 21, we want everyone to know. It is so important the brand name is put on the front of garments for the world to see. But the most important label is the one which says, "Made by Almighty God." Remember YOU are important - God breathed His very breath into YOU and you became a living soul. Act like it. God bless.

Day 27: As for man, his days are like grass; he flourishes like a flower of the field." (Psalm) We are to grow up and we are to flourish (prosper and increase). We are not made to sit around and live a sedentary (stagnant, sluggish) life. We cannot expect to flourish if we will not get up and get moving. Our society lends itself to living life by doing as little as possible. Shakepeare said, "Nothing will come of nothing." We just might evolve with a bigger 'tush,' larger hands, smaller legs and feet because of our chosen lifestyle. Utilizing what is ours is a God thing. Make sure you flourish like the flower, bring beauty, and multiply so that you can give increase to the world in which you live. God bless.

Day 28: We are made to work, to take action. The way to take action is to believe in oneself and to believe it is possible to achieve what we want to achieve. To increase belief in oneself and the possibilities of life, one must surround oneself with those who believe in you and read books that will encourage you to keep believing. (Bible) By doing so, your faith to make the impossible possible will increase. God bless.

Day 29: Wouldn't it be awesome if the world was truthful. My email has just been hacked by those trying to make a dishonest buck. If they would use their intelligence to add good to the world and to help others, it would be a better place in which to live. May God show them the error of their ways because they will truly reap what they have sown and Lord have mercy on their souls. God bless.

Day 30: There is one thing we can depend on ~ CHANGE. If we want the change, we are good with it; but if not, it can be scary. Change is all around: age brings change, circumstances change, people in our lives change, our jobs change, bosses change, world dynamics change and all of this happens without OUR permission. *One thing is for sure, God stays the same. He is the same yesterday, today, and forever, Learn to lean on, trust in, and depend upon Him and His Son. He will see you through every change victoriously. God bless.

Works Cited

Bible Hub. www.Biblehub.com

Brainy Quote. www.brainyquote.com

Byrne, Rhonda. The Secret. New York: Atria Books, 2006.

Meyer, Joyce. *Trusting God day by day*. New York: Faith Words, 2012.

Osteen, Joel. *I Declare*. New York: Faith Words, 2012.

Our Daily Bread Ministeries. www.ourdailybread.org.

ABOUT THE AUTHOR

Peggy was born in Cookeville, Tennessee, and lived there until she finished her college education at Tennessee Technological University with a Secondary Education degree. Her first teaching job was in Black Mountain, NC, and then in Winder, GA, before the family moved to Thessaloniki, Greece, where she lived for five years teaching at Pinewood Schools. She has taught public school for 43 years and is on her 33rd year teaching on the collegiate level. Her English classroom was a den of stories and life lessons. "A doctor may save a life, but a teacher can help make someone's life worth living," was her motto.

If that wasn't enough, she has taken people of all ages around the world, on six continents, for over 43 years and continues to do so She has also embraced storytelling and has told at the Swapping Ground in Jonesborough, TN, the StoryFest in the Park in Cookeville, as well as private appearances. . "Stories embrace the human heart, connect and heal the human spirit." She authored *That's the Truth If I Ever Told It,* a biography about Bashful Brother Oswald, a Grand Ole Opry legend. She continues living in Cookeville while visiting her children and friends whenever the opportunity comes.

Made in the USA
Lexington, KY
13 December 2016